Eugenio Fascetti • Romedio Scaia

D1037798

SOCCER
Attacking Schemes
and Training Exercises

Library of Congress Cataloging - in - Publication Data

Fascetti, Eugenio and Scaia, Romedio
  Soccer - Attacking Schemes and Training Exercises

ISBN No. 1-890946-15-X
Library of Congress Catalog Card Number 98-065648
Copyright © May 1998

Reedswain books are available at special discounts for bulk purchase. For details, contact the Reedswain at 1-800-331-5191.

Art Direction, Design and Layout
Kimberly N. Bender
Editing and Proofing
Bryan R. Beaver

Printed by
DATA REPRODUCTIONS
Auburn Hills, Michigan

REEDSWAIN BOOKS and VIDEOS
612 Pughtown Road
Spring City, Pennsylvania 19475 USA
1-800-331-5191 • www.reedswain.com

Foreword

I thought it would be a useful thing to put together in one book many of the attacking schemes and exercises which I have used and written down in my experience as a coach.

At first I wanted to make a strict selection and give them a precise order according to their content, degree of difficulty, number and role of the players involved etc.

But then I thought that in this way I could induce a schematic and inflexible mental state, which any coach and player should absolutely avoid.

So, I opted for grouping them according to their themes: the forwards' and/or the midfielders' criss-crossing, overlapping on the sides, counter-attack, and so on.

Virtually, I left them to the inventiveness and insight of the moment in order to give that idea of mental flexibility which, in my opinion, is the key to any successful tactical scheme.

However good and effective a scheme may be, it will always be something repetitive and mechanical: this is why I think it is useful if applied in order to acquire those rational attitudes (in particular in the definition of roles) needed to maintain the tactical balance in a team. On the contrary, if we use a scheme as an unquestionable rule which everybody must strictly obey we will suppress the genius of the individual player and spontaneous play: and then, farewell to the beautiful soccer game.

Eugenio Fascetti

Table of Contents

Key

2	Defending player
. . . . ▸	Movement of the Defending Player
2	Initial position of the player to coach
2	Final position of the player to coach
⟶	Trajectory of the ball
– – ⇢	Movement without the ball
⌇⌇⌇➤	Dribbling the ball
(2	Screen of the defender

Exercises for Overlapping a Defender

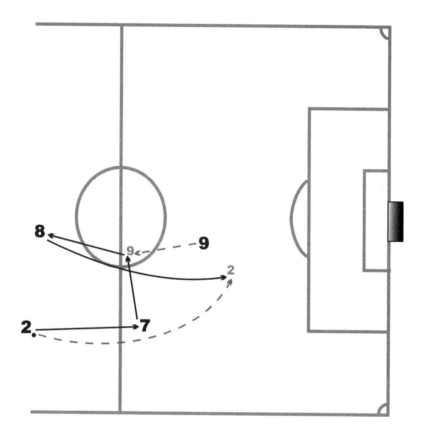

BASIC EXERCISE

The exercise starts with the four players in an attacking situation, without the backs:

- 2 passes the ball to 7;
- 7 passes the ball to 9 who has come towards him;
- 9 passes the ball to 8;
- 8 passes the ball to 2 who has inserted himself into the wing, overlapping 7.

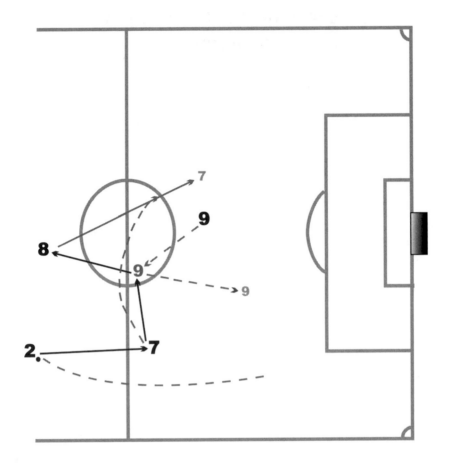

FIRST VARIATION

- 2 passes the ball to 7 and then overlaps on the wing;
- 7 passes the ball to 9 who has come towards him;
- 9 passes the ball to 8 and then makes a quick cut, as if he wants to receive the pass from 8;
- 8, instead, passes the ball to 7 who has moved into the center.

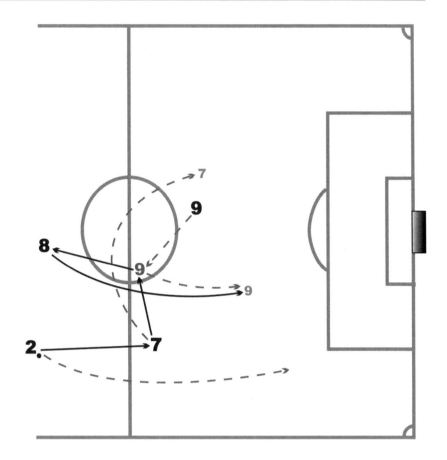

SECOND VARIATION

- 2 passes the ball to 7 and then overlaps on the wing;
- 7 passes to 9 who has come towards him;
- 9 passes to 8;
- 7 overlaps 9, as if he wants to receive the pass from 8;
- instead, 8 passes the ball to 9 who is ready to receive the pass thanks to a quick turn.

Exercises for Overlapping a Defender with Opposition

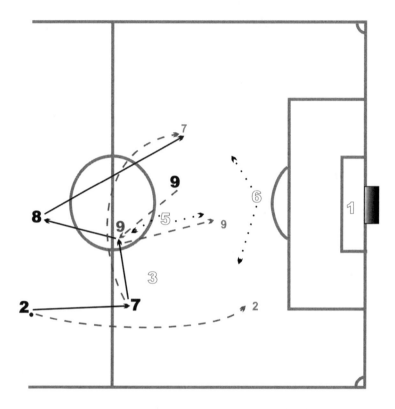

Now let's do both the basic exercise and the two variations also with the goalkeeper and three backs: back 5 and back 3 are partially active, while sweeper 6, active, tries to challenge - in turn - player 2, or 7 or 9: they may either dribble or shoot at goal immediately.
Then, backs 3 and 5 become active and depending on their choices we will know which scheme to adopt.

We will adopt the BASIC SCHEME if, when player 8 has the ball, back 3 man-marks player 7 and back 5 follows player 9.

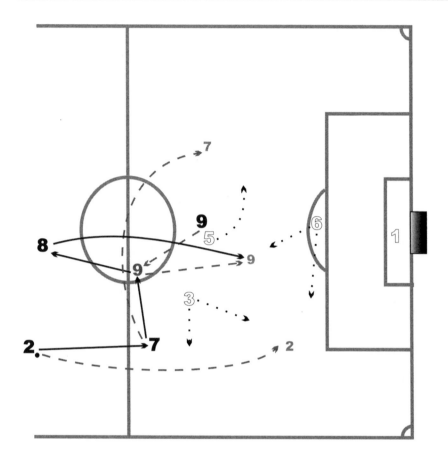

We will adopt the FIRST VARIATION if back 3 opts for zone-marking player 2.

Finally, we will adopt the SECOND VARIATION if back 5, noticing the forward movement of player 7, gets away from player 9 to help back 6.

Scheme to Set Free a Back on the Weak Side Wing, Opposite to the One Where the Play is Started

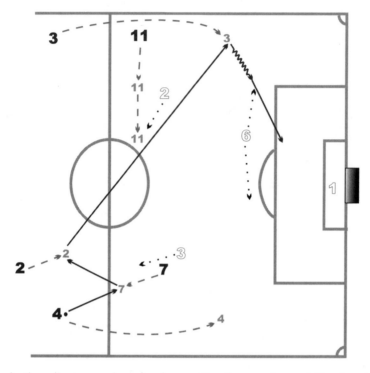

Though the diagram already shows the forwards and the backs, they are introduced later: first the exercise must be carried out without the backs, only with the goalkeeper.

- 4 passes the ball to 7 (who has come towards him) and then moves down the right wing;
- 2 moves forward to receive the ball from 7;
- 3 overlaps 11 on the left wing;
- 11 makes a "dummy" run inside and distracts his own marking player;
- 2 makes a long pass to 3, who advances and shoots at goal.

Scheme to Set Free a back on the Weak Side Wing, Opposite to the One Where the Play is Started, with Change of Position According to the Reaction of the Backs.

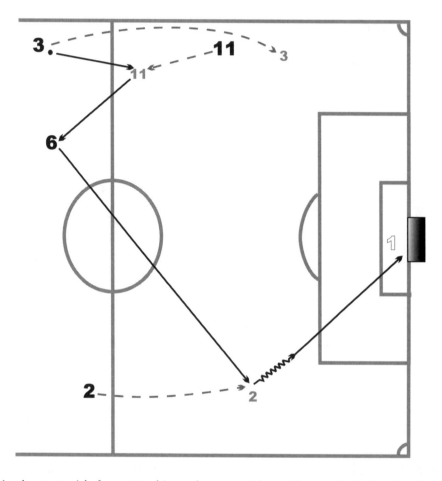

Let's start with four attacking players, without the backs but with the goalkeeper:

- 3 passes the ball to 11 (who comes towards him) and overlaps down the wing;
- 11 passes the ball to 6;
- 6 makes a long pass to 2 who has moved down the opposite wing;
- 2 advances, then shoots from just outside the penalty area.

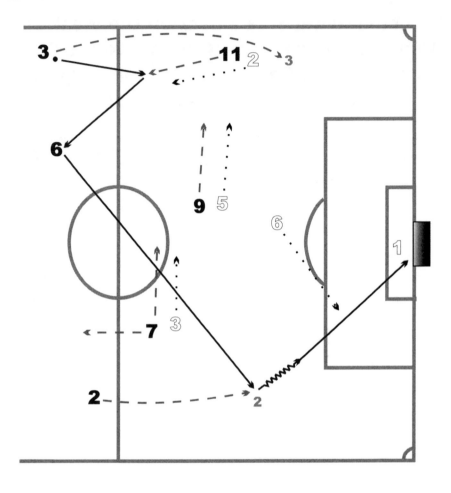

Now let's add two forwards (9 and 7), three marking backs (3, 5, 2) and a sweeper (6).

The sweeper is half-active: he can only challenge player 2's shots. Backs 3, 5, 2 must follow the movements made by their direct opponents.

The scheme is the same, but 7 and 9 must "take away" backs 3 and 5, so that 6 can make a long pass to 2.

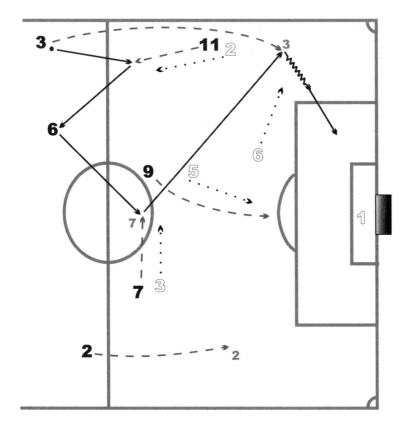

Now let's make a variation, without changing either positions or defensive tasks:

- 3 passes the ball to 11 (who comes towards him) and overlaps down the wing;
- 2 moves down the opposite wing;
- 11 passes the ball to 6;
- 6 passes the ball to 7 who has come towards him to receive the pass;
- 3 goes ahead in his overlapping movement on the wing;
- 9 distracts his own marking player;
- 7 makes a long pass to 3;
- 3 receives the pass, advances and then shoots.

Later, the backs can be allowed to be free to choose, so that the forwards can opt for either scheme, depending on the choice of the backs.

Exercise to Create Superiority in Numbers on the Wing

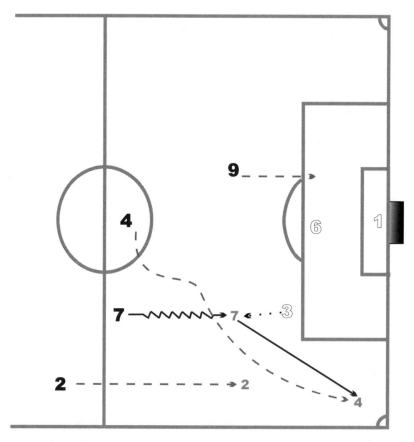

Here we have four attacking players (2, 4, 7, 9) against back 3 and sweeper 6, who is passive:

- 7 starts from the midfield with the ball, advances and then dribbles directly towards back 3 who is facing him;
- at this point 2 and 4 must support 7;
- 2 feints to go down the right wing, where 4 actually overlaps.

This movement will enable 7 to have two solutions, depending of course on the decision made by back 3:
  a. if 3 decides to tackle forward 7 directly, the latter will pass the ball to his overlapping teammate 4;

b. however, if 3 decides to zone mark the overlapping of player 4, then 7 will keep the ball and go towards the goal.

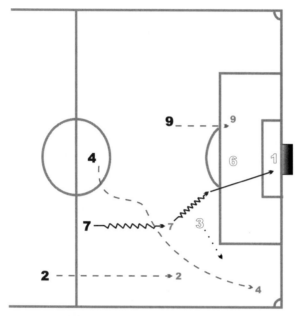

Later, when sweeper 6 becomes active, there will be other solutions:
- 7 may pass the ball to 4, who cross-passes to 9;
- 7 may pass the ball directly to 9.

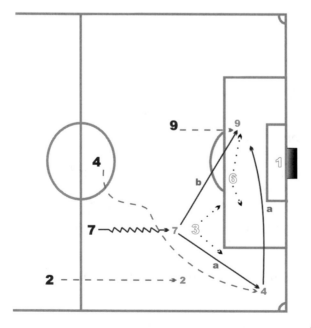

Double Overlapping Between the Back and the Wing

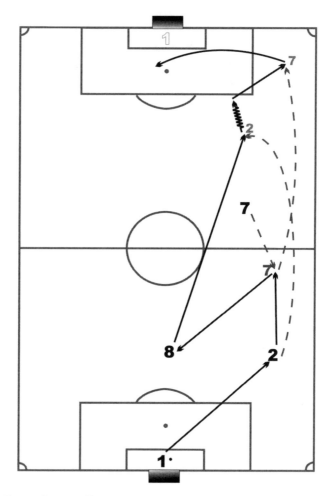

Let's start from the goalkeeper:
- 1 passes the ball to 2;
- 2 passes the ball to 7 who has come towards him, and then overlaps down the wing;
- 7 passes the ball to 8, then he overlaps 2;
- 8 makes a long pass to 2, who advances with the ball for a short distance waiting for 7 to arrive, then he passes 7 the ball.

The exercise must be performed like this for a few times.

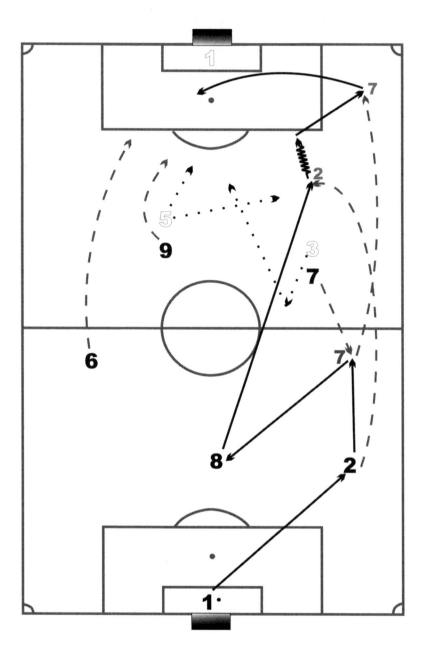

Later, we can add two forwards (6 and 9) and two active backs (3 and 5). Finally, the number of the defenders can be increased.

Overlapping Exercise for Crosses and Finishing

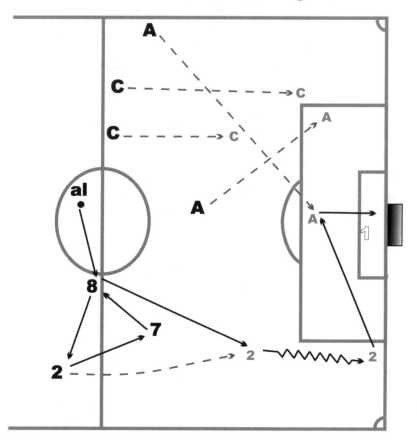

This exercise is carried out by:
I.   two midfielders (7 and 8);
II. one back (2);
III. and, optionally, other midfielders (C), one or more forwards (A) and a goalkeeper (1):

- the coach (al), or player C, passes the ball to 8;
- 8 passes the ball to 2;
- 2 passes the ball to 7 and then overlaps down the wing;
- 7 passes the ball to 8, who passes it to 2;
- 2 dribbles towards the endline and then crosses the ball;
- the additional forwards and midfielders can criss-cross and in turns receive the pass to shoot at goal.

Possible variations:
- 2 can receive the ball from 8 coming towards him;
- 7 can receive the ball from 2 coming towards him;
- 8 can receive the ball from 7 coming towards him or making a slightly diagonal move towards the center.

The exercise must also be performed on the left side of the field. Later, the backs must be added: first passive, then semi-active, finally active.

An alternative is to add three backs, of whom only the sweeper is active at first.

Exercise for Overlapping Midfielders

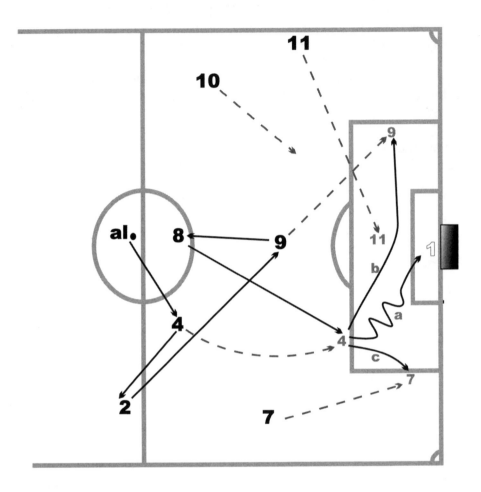

This simple exercise is carried out by:
I.   two midfielders (4 and 8);
II. one back (2);
III. one forward (9);
IV. and, optionally, another midfielder (10), one or more forwards (11) and a goalkeeper (1):

- the coach (al), or a player, passes the ball to 4;
- 4 passes the ball to 2 and overlaps into an attacking position;
- 2 makes a long pass to 9;
- 9 back-passes to 8, who makes a long pass to 4;

- 4 has three options. He can:
  a. go directly towards the goal;
  b. pass the ball to forward 11 or 9, who have criss-crossed;
  c. pass the ball to forward 7, who supports him on the right.

The exercise must also be performed on the left side of the field.

Later, the backs must be added: first passive, then semi-active, finally active.

An alternative is to add three backs, of whom only the sweeper is active at first.

Exercise Enabling a Midfielder to Cut in During the Final Phase

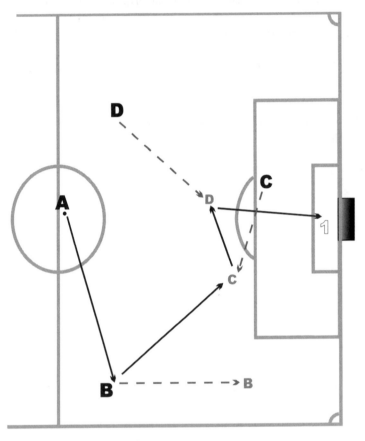

This exercise is carried out by:

I.   one back (A);
II. two midfielders (B and D);
III. one forward (C);
IV. a goalkeeper (1):

- while A passes to B, C comes towards B to receive an eventual pass;
- B passes the ball to C and then sprints down the right wing, feinting to be ready to receive the pass from C;
- instead, C passes the ball to D who has come forward and shoots directly at goal.

The exercise must also be performed on the left side of the field.

Scheme Enabling a Midfielder to Cut in During the Final Phase

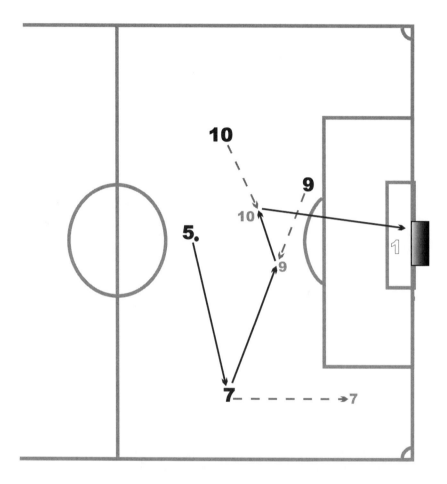

This exercise is carried out by four players who arrange themselves as shown in the above diagram.
5 is the player with the ball:

- 5 passes the ball to 7;
- 9 comes towards him to receive the pass;
- 7 passes the ball to 9;
- 10 makes a diagonal move;
- 9 passes the ball to 10;
- 10 shoots at goal;
- 7 moves down the right wing, in order to support an eventual variation.

Exercise for Getting into the Central Area

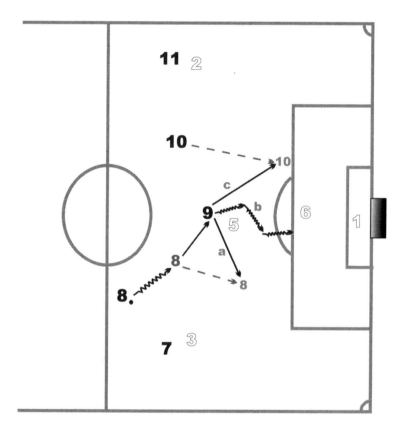

Here we have two midfielders (8 and 10), two forwards (9 and 11) and one linkman (7) against four defenders (2, 5, 6, 3).

Player 8 advances with the ball for a short distance then passes it to 9, who has three options, he can:

    a. pass it to 8, who has kept on running after passing the ball.

    b. try to dribble past stopper 5 and go towards the goal.

    c. pass the ball to 10 who has moved into the central area on his left.

Sweeper 6 may be indecisive, as he does not know what space to close down.

Players 11 and 7 must keep their marking players 2 and 3 busy.

Exercise for Getting into the Central Area

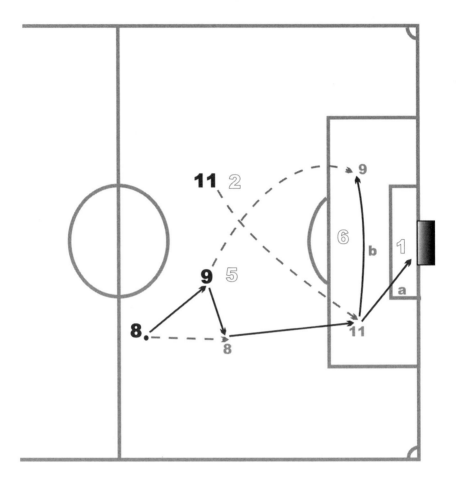

One midfielder (8) and two forwards (9 and 11) play against three backs (2, 6, 5):

- player 8 passes the ball to 9, then moves forward and receives the ball;
- meanwhile, player 11 has moved forward diagonally and receives the ball from 8;
- 9 cuts into the opposite side of the penalty area;
- 11 has two options: he can:
    - a. shoot at goal directly;
    - b. make a cross-pass to the center for player 9.

Scheme for the Overlapping of a Side Back on the Right Wing, with Criss-Crossing Between a Forward and a Midfielder

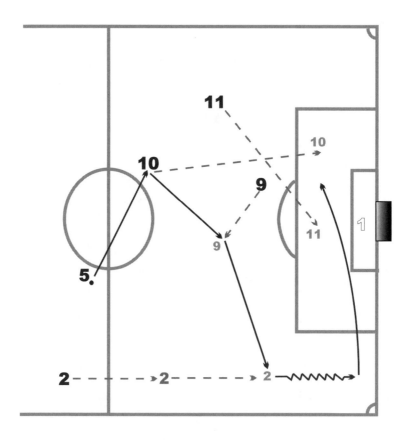

This exercise is carried out by five players who arrange themselves as shown in the above diagram.
5 is the player with the ball:
- 5 passes the ball to 10;
- 2 moves down the wing;
- 9 comes backward to receive the pass;
- 10 passes the ball to 9 and moves into the penalty area, criss-crossing with 11 who carries out the same movement;
- 9 passes the ball to 2;
- 2 goes towards the end of the field and then crosses the ball to either 10 or 11.

Scheme for Getting onto the Wing, with Double Overlapping Between the Side Back and a Midfielder, with a Shot at Goal by the Other Midfielder

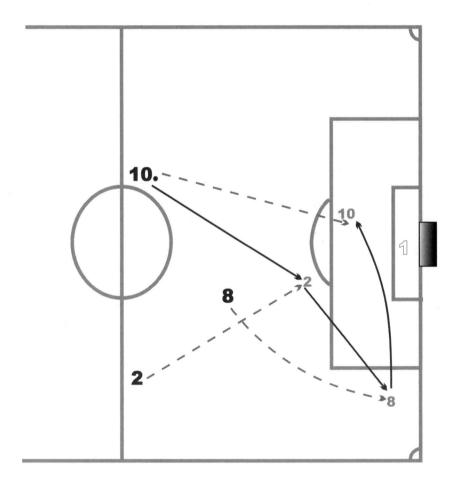

The exercise is carried out by three players.
10 is the player with the ball:

- 2 overlaps 8;
- 10 passes the ball to 2, while 8 overlaps 2;
- 2 passes the ball to 8, while 10 gets into the penalty area;
- 8 crosses the ball to 10.

Scheme for the Overlapping of a Midfielder on the Wing and Criss-Crossing of the Forwards to Shoot at Goal

This exercise is carried out by five players.
6 is the player with the ball:

- 6 passes the ball to 10;
- 10 passes it to 9 who has come backward;
- 8 overlaps 10 on the right wing;
- 9 makes a long pass to 8 and then criss-crosses with 11;
- 8 crosses to either 11 or 9, who shoot at goal.

Scheme for Getting a Back onto the Wing, with a Forward and a Midfielder Criss-Crossing, and the Penetration of Another Midfielder in the Center of the Attack

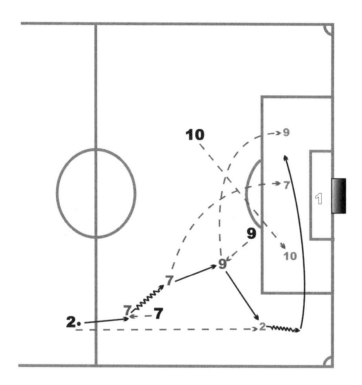

BASIC SCHEME
- 2 passes the ball to 7 (who has come towards him) and then overlaps down the right wing;
- 7 passes the ball to 9 who has come towards him;
- 9 passes the ball to 2;
- 9 and 10 criss-cross;
- 7 penetrates into the center of the attack,
- 2 moves forward with the ball, then crosses to 9, 7 or 10.

Special attention should be paid to the timing of the criss-crossing between 9 and 10 (which must take place first) and the penetration run of 7 which must take place immediately afterwards.
In such a situation it is up to 7 to choose the right moment for his run.

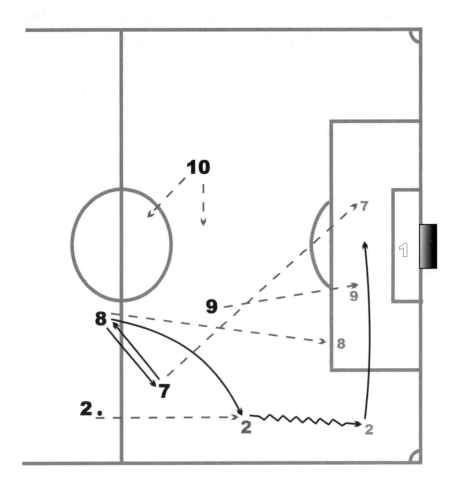

FIRST VARIATION

- the exercise starts with a pass and a return pass between 8 and 7;
- 2 gets into the wing, overlapping 7;
- 8 passes the ball to 2;
- 7, 8 and 9 run forward;
- 2 goes towards the end of the field with the ball, then cross-passes to 7, 8 or 9.

The timing of the criss-crossing between 7 and 8 (which must take place first) and between 7 and 9 (which must take place immediately afterwards) is very important.

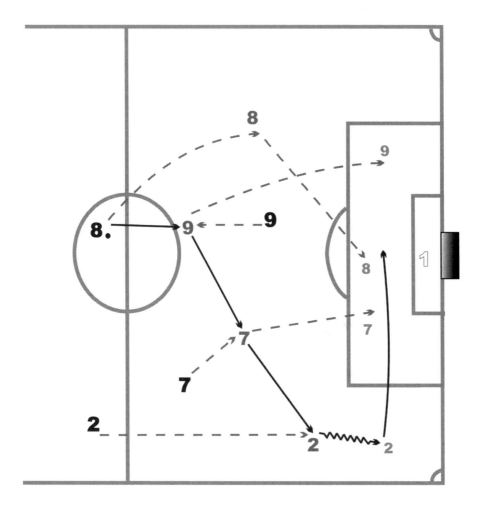

SECOND VARIATION

- 8 passes the ball to 9 (who has come towards him) and then runs quickly forward;
- 2 moves quickly into the right wing;
- 9 passes the ball to 7 (who has moved forward to receive the pass) and then gets into the penalty area, criss-crossing with 8;
- 7 passes the ball to 2, then gets into the penalty area;
- 2 goes towards the end of the field with the ball, then cross-passes to 9, 8 or 7.

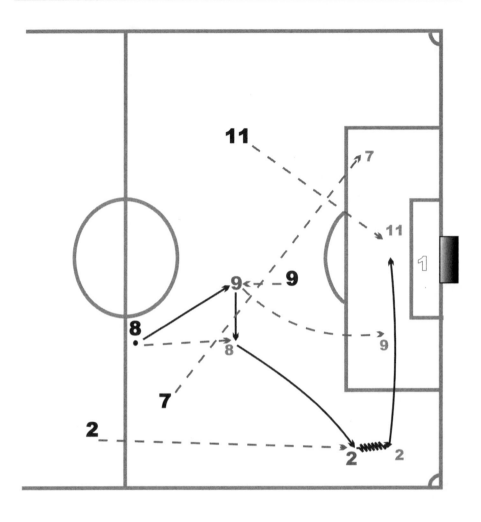

THIRD VARIATION

There is a second forward (11) instead of the midfielder.

- 8 passes the ball to 9 who has come towards him;
- 9 passes the ball back to 8 who has moved forward in triangulation;
- 2 gets onto the right wing;
- 8 feints to pass the ball to 7, instead he passes it to 2;
- 7 and 9 run forward and criss-cross;
- so does 11;
- 2 goes towards the end of the field, then cross-passes to 11, 9 or 7;
- 8 stays behind to cover.

Scheme for the Overlapping of a Midfielder on the Wing and Criss-Crossing of the Forwards to Shoot at Goal

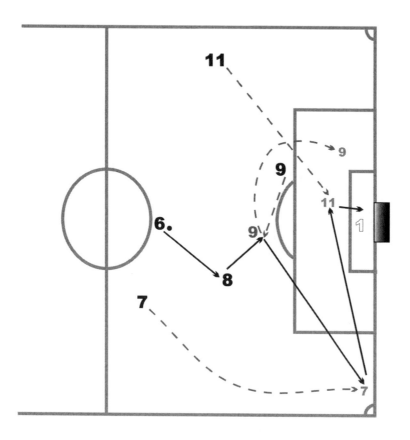

The exercise is carried out by five players:
I.   defender 6;
II. midfielders 8 and 7;
III. forwards 9 and 11:

- 6 passes the ball to 8;
- 8 passes the ball to 9, who has come towards him;
- 7 gets onto the wing and gets the pass from 9;
- 9 criss-crosses with 11;
- 7 cross-passes either to 9 or 11 (try both passes).

Then, the exercise should be carried out on the left wing.

Attacking Scheme with Penetration from Behind of the Midfielder who takes Advantage of the Criss-Crossing with the Forward

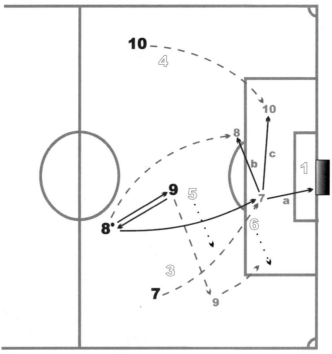

Here we have four attacking players (7, 8, 9, 10) and four defenders (4, 5, 6, 3).

8 is the player with the ball:

- quick exchange 8 to 9, 9 to 8;
- 9 moves diagonally to the side followed by stopper 5 and sweeper 6;
- 7 criss-crosses with 9. This movement must be made very quickly, in order to leave back 3 behind;
- 8 passes the ball to 7 and gets into the attack;
- 10 moves to the left side of the penalty area.

Now 7 has three options, he can:

    a. shoot at goal;
    b. pass the ball to 8;
    c. pass the ball to 10.

Attacking Scheme with Penetration from Behind of the Midfielder, who takes Advantage of the Criss-Crossing Between the Forward and the Other Midfielder

Here we have four attacking players (7, 8, 9, 10) and four defenders (4, 5, 6, 3).

8 is the player with the ball:

- quick exchange 8 to 7, 7 to 8;
- 8 goes forward with the ball towards sweeper 6;
- 9 and 7 criss-cross, followed by their marking players;
- 10 moves into the left side of the penalty area.

Now 8 has three options, he can:

- a. dribble past 6 and shoot at goal;
- b. pass the ball to 7;
- c. pass the ball to 10.

There can be variations in the final phase:

- 7 and 10 can criss-cross;
- 7 can screen back 4, releasing 10.

Exercise for the Penetration of a Midfielder Overlapping on the Wing

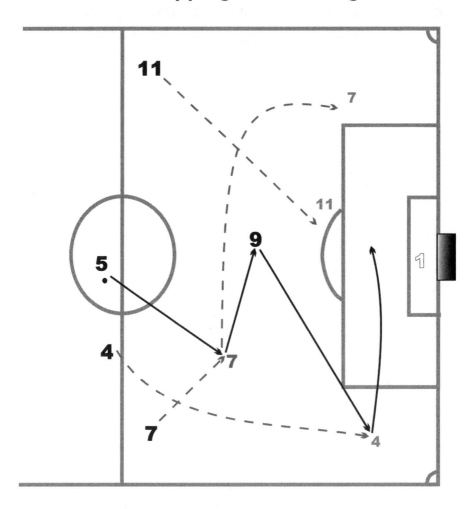

The exercise is carried out by players 5, 7, 4, 9, and 11.
5 is the player with the ball.

- 5 passes the ball to 7 who "cuts in" in order to get the pass;
- 7 passes the ball to 9;
- 4 overlaps on the wing;
- 7 criss-crosses with 11 and moves onto the left wing;
- 9 makes a long pass to 4, who cross-passes to 11 and 7.

Overlapping on the Wing, Cut-ins and Criss-Crossings

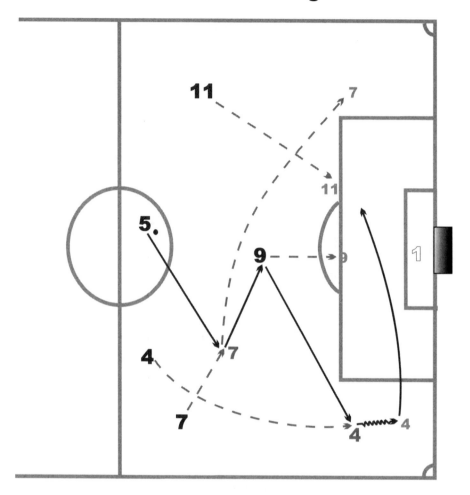

- 5 passes the ball to 7 who "cuts in" in order to get the pass;
- 4 overlaps on the right wing, criss-crossing the cut-in by 7;
- 7 passes the ball to 9 and then criss-crosses with 11;
- 9 passes the ball to 4 and goes quickly towards the penalty area;
- 4 advances with the ball for a short distance, then cross-passes to 9, 7, 11.

Overlapping of a Back on the Wing and Penetration of a Midfielder to Shoot

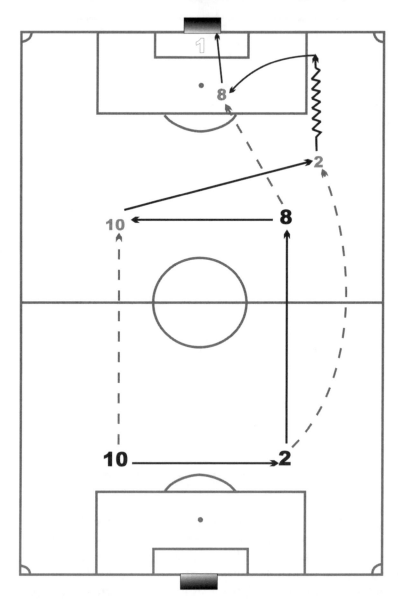

- 10 passes the ball to 2 and runs forward beyond the midfield;
- 2 makes a forward pass to 8 and then overlaps on the right wing;
- 8 passes the ball to 10 and cuts diagonally into the penalty area;
- 10 makes a diagonal pass to 2, who advances with the ball towards the end of the field and then makes a cross-pass to 8.

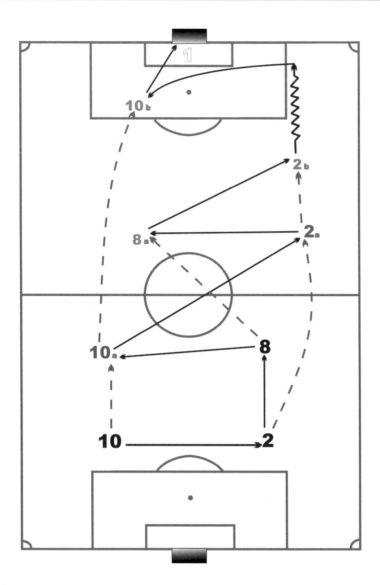

VARIATION to the same scheme.
Insertion of the other midfielder:

- 10 passes the ball to 2 and goes to position 10a;
- 2 makes a forward pass to 8 and overlaps onto position 2a;
- 8 passes the ball to 10 and overlaps onto position 8a;
- 10 makes a diagonal pass to 2, who immediately makes a lateral pass to 8 and goes quickly to position 2b to get the return pass;
- meanwhile 10 has reached position 10b;
- after getting the ball back from 8, 2 advances towards the end of the field and makes a cross-pass to 10.

Passing from the Wing to Shoot at Goal

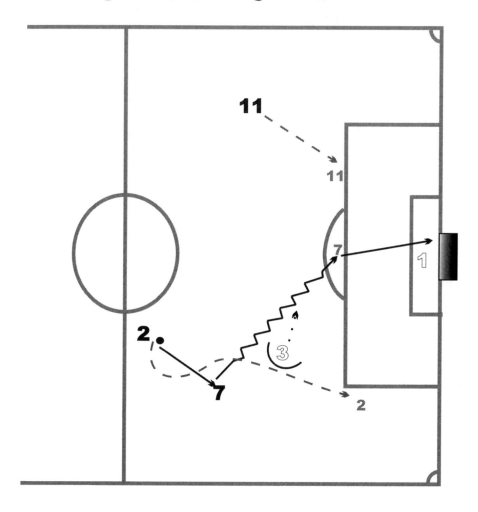

- 2 passes the ball to 7 and feints to overlap; instead, he quickly changes his direction and passes by 7 in order to screen or block back 3;
- 7 advances with the ball, then shoots directly at goal;
- 11 follows the action on the other side.

Passing from the Wing to Shoot at Goal

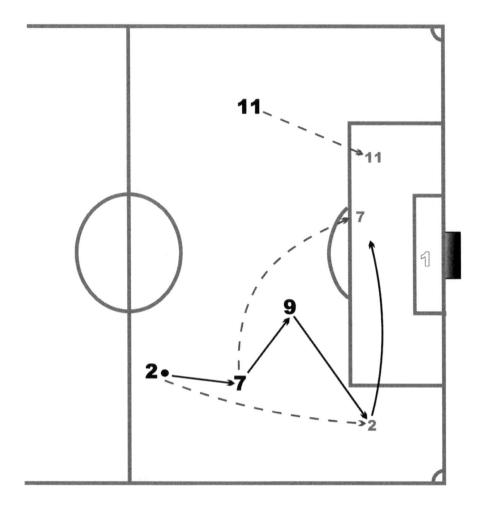

- 2 passes the ball to 7 and overlaps on the right wing;
- 7 passes the ball to 9 and moves into the center, as if he were to get the ball back;
- 11 "cuts in" from the left;
- 9 passes the ball to 2, who immediately cross-passes to 7.

Passes Between the Forwards

Here we can see that:

- 8 passes the ball to 11 who has "cut" sideways in order to get the pass;
- 9 moves diagonally to the left into the penalty area;
- 7 gets onto the right wing;
- 6 moves diagonally forward towards the center;
- 11 passes the ball to 7, who cross-passes to 9.

VARIATION

When 11 gets the ball, 7 feints an insertion on the wing and then cuts in towards the center: he gets the pass from 11, advances with the ball for a short distance, then shoots at goal.

Of course, the choice between the "basic option" and the "variation" depends on the movement made by player 7.

Passing in the Midfield with Penetration on the Wing

These exercises are particularly helpful in a 4.4.2 arrangement, and are extremely useful to reach a more and more accurate timing.
They must be carried out at maximum speed.

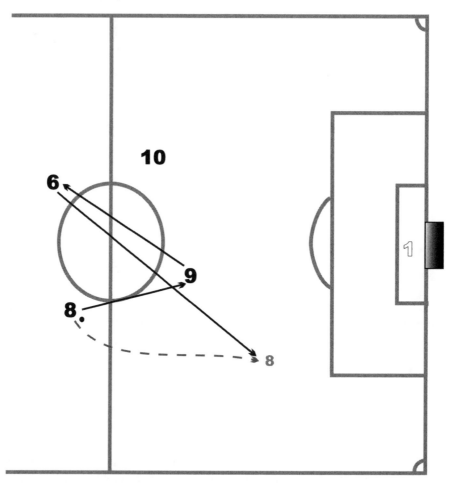

- 8 passes the ball to 9 and overlaps;
- 9 passes the ball to 6;
- 6 makes a long pass to 8.

Now let's see the same exercise on the left:
- 6 passes the ball to 10 and overlaps;
- 10 passes the ball to 8;
- 8 makes a long pass to 6.

First, the exercise is carried out without the backs and without shooting at goal.

Then, the following defenders are added:
- backs 5 and 4 (marking 9 and 10 respectively);
- sweeper 6;
- the goalkeeper: in this case there is a shot at goal.

The backs are passive at first, then become semi-active and finally active.

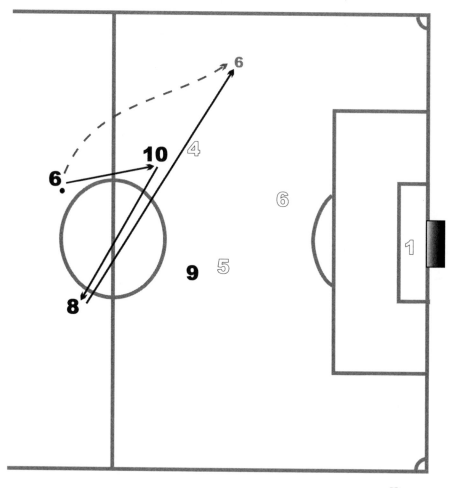

Criss-Crossing Between the Forward and the Midfielder Passing in the Midfield

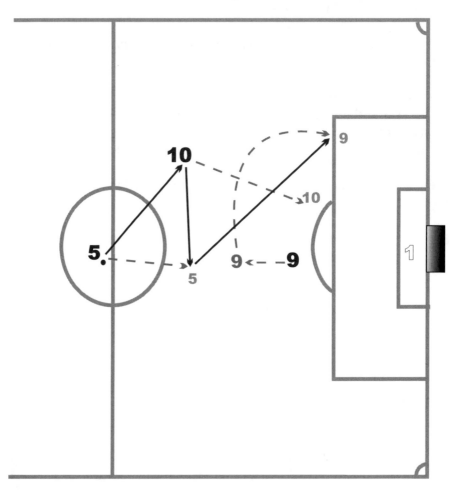

The exercise is carried out by three players: 5, 10, 9:

- 5 passes the ball to 10, then runs forwards to get the return pass;
- 10 passes the ball back to 5;
- at this moment, 9 takes some steps towards the ball as if he were to get the pass; instead, he makes a quick turn and runs forward, criss-crossing with 10 who gets into the center of the attack;
- 5 can pass the ball to either 9 or 10.

FIRST VARIATION

5 might not be in a position to pass the ball to either 9 or 10 (as they might be marked appropriately by the backs).

In this case he will try to keep possession of the ball and start a new scheme, which might be the following:

- 5 passes the ball to 10 and then advances slowly;
- 10 passes the ball to 9, who has come towards him, and then overlaps him to give the impression that he wants to get the ball back;
- instead, 9 makes a long pass to 5, who has now sprinted quickly in deep.
- 10 continues his movement towards the penalty area;
- 9 stays behind.

Later, an active back and a goalkeeper can be added to create other solutions.

For example:

a. 5 advances with the ball, tries to beat the back 1 on 1 and shoots from the edge of the penalty area;

b. pressured by the back, 5 passes the ball to 10 who shoots at goal;

c. pressured by the back, 5 passes the ball to 10 and advances to get the eventual cross pass from 10.

SECOND VARIATION

Let's add a fourth player (7):

- 5 is the player with the ball;
- 7 comes towards him and gets the pass;
- 9 feints that he wants to get the pass from 7: he comes backward for some yards, but then he turns suddenly and goes towards the penalty area, where he gets the pass from 10 who, meanwhile, has received the ball from 7.

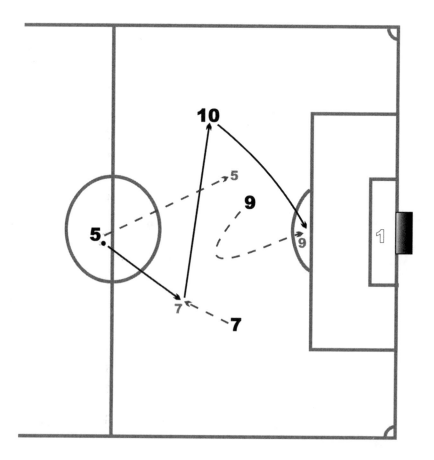

THIRD VARIATION

A more complex variation of this scheme (with the criss-crossing of the two midfielders):

- 5 passes the ball to 7;
- 7 passes the ball to 9 who has come towards him;
- 9 passes the ball back to 5 who has come forward;
- 7 and 10 criss-cross;
- 5 passes the ball to 7 (but he could also make a long pass to 10).

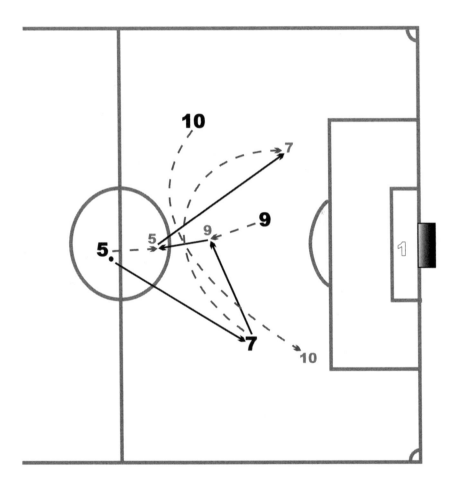

Penetration of a Midfielder onto the Wing Passing Beyond the Midfield

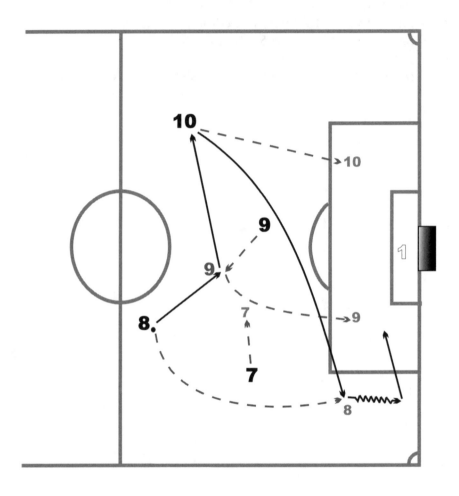

- 8 passes the ball to 9, who has come towards him;
- 9 feints to pass the ball to 7 (who has moved towards the center), instead he passes to 10;
- 8 gets quickly onto the right wing, overlapping 7 who stays behind;
- 10 makes a long pass to 8 and runs towards the penalty area;
- so does 9;
- 8 advances with the ball for a short distance, then cross-passes to either 9 or 10.

Criss-Crossing of the Midfielder and of the Forward with Penetration of Another Midfielder onto the Wing, Passing Beyond the Midfield

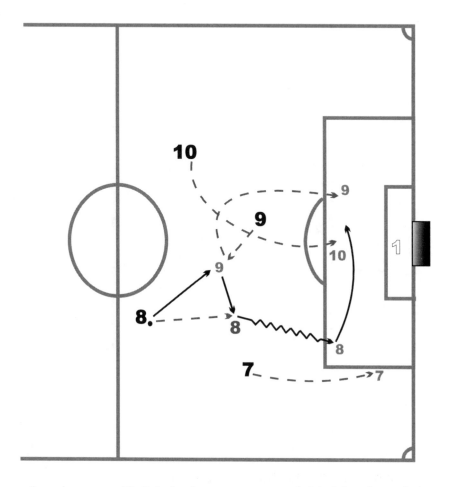

- 8 exchanges with 9 (who has come towards him) in triangulation, then advances with the ball for a short distance;
- 9 and 10 criss-cross;
- 8 cross-passes to either 9 or 10;
- 7 supports 8 on the right for an eventual pass: he could get the pass from 8 and cross-pass.

Penetration of the Midfielder and Criss-Crossing with the Forward Passing in the Midfield

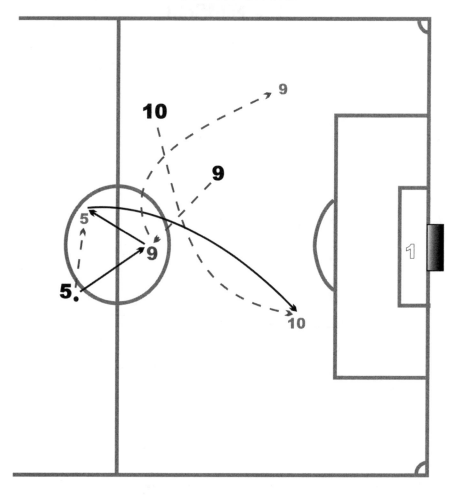

This exercise aims at achieving good timing.

- 5 passes the ball to 9 (who has come towards him) and moves diagonally to get the return pass;
- 9 passes the ball back to 5;
- 10 sprints in deep to the right, criss-crossing with 9 who does the same thing from the opposite side;
- 5 can choose to pass the ball to either 9 or 10.

VARIATION

- 5 passes the ball to 9 (who has come towards him) and moves diagonally to get the return pass;
- 9 feints a pass to 5, instead he passes the ball to 10;
- 5 continues his movement, overlapping on the left;
- 9 moves slightly backwards.

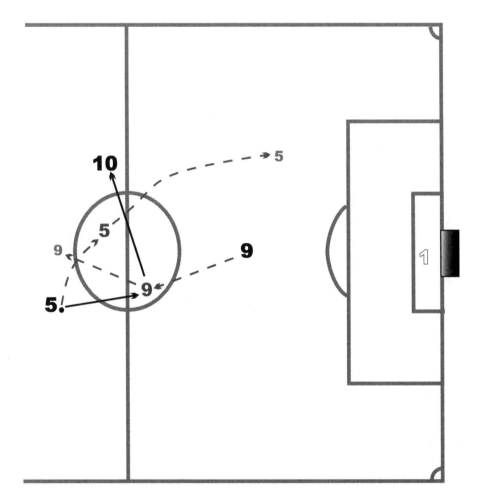

Now 10 has three options, he can:
   a. make a pass to 5 who has moved into the attack;
   b. advance towards the goal;
   c. pass the ball to 9 and sprint forward to get the pass from his teammate.

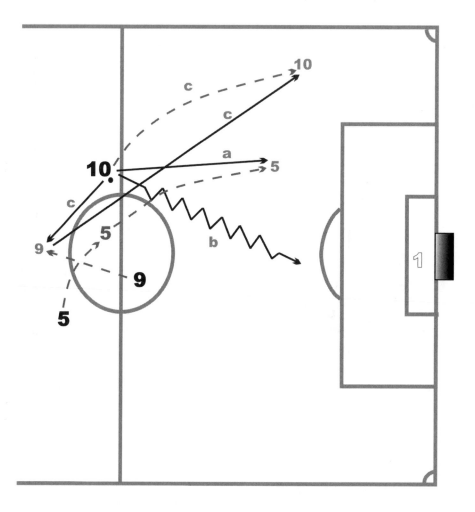

This exercise must be carried out first just with the forwards, then with the backs (whose number is optional) and the goalkeeper, in order to end up with a shot at goal.

Cut-ins and Criss-Crossings in the Midfield in Order to Free a Teammate Along the Wing

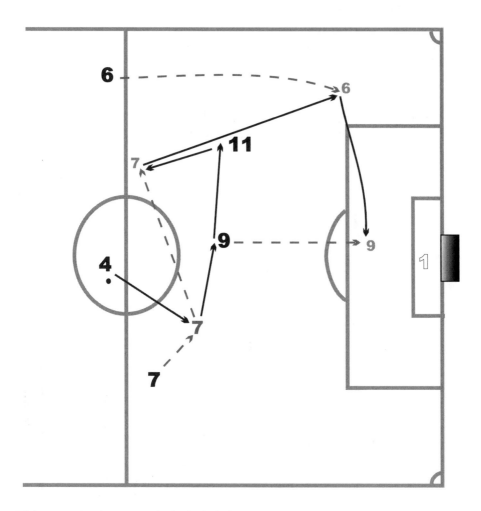

This exercise is particularly helpful in a 4:4:2 arrangement.

It is carried out by five players: 7, 4, 9, 11, 6:

- 4 passes the ball to 7 who has moved diagonally to get the pass;
- 7 passes the ball to 9, who 'dummies' and lets the ball reach 11;
- 11 passes the ball back to 7, who meanwhile has moved diagonally backwards to the left;
- 6 sprints down the left wing;
- 7 passes the ball to 6 who cross-passes to 9, who meanwhile has moved forward into the center of the attack.

We can see the same exercise in the diagram below, carried out on the other side by six players as we have added side back 2.

4 is the player with the ball:

- 7 moves diagonally forward to get the pass;
- 4 passes the ball to him;
- 7 passes it to 9, who makes a dummy movement and lets the ball reach 11;
- meanwhile, 2 has quickly overlapped 7 on the right wing;
- 11 makes a long pass to 2, who advances and then cross-passes;
- 6, 9 and 11 move forward to get the pass.

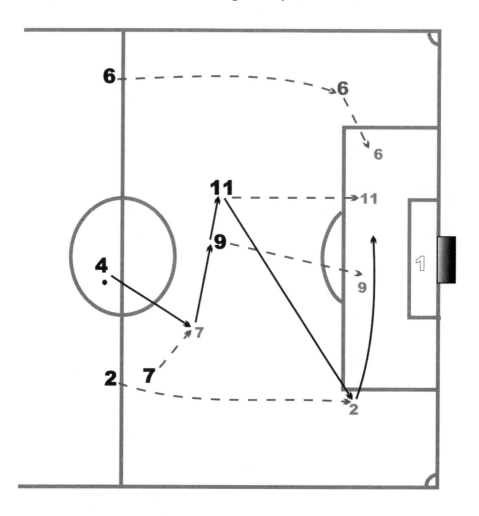

Now let's see a variation of the same scheme.
The number of players is the same, with player 8 instead of 4:

- 7 moves diagonally forward to get the pass;
- 8 passes the ball to him;
- 7 passes it to 9;
- 9 passes it back to 7 (who has moved diagonally backwards to get the pass) and then sprints forward;
- 2 overlaps 7 on the right wing;
- 6 sprints onto the left wing;
- 7 makes a pass to 11, who has criss-crossed with 9;
- 11 can:
  a. advance and shoot at goal;
  b. pass the ball to 2, who can cross-pass to either 9 or 6.

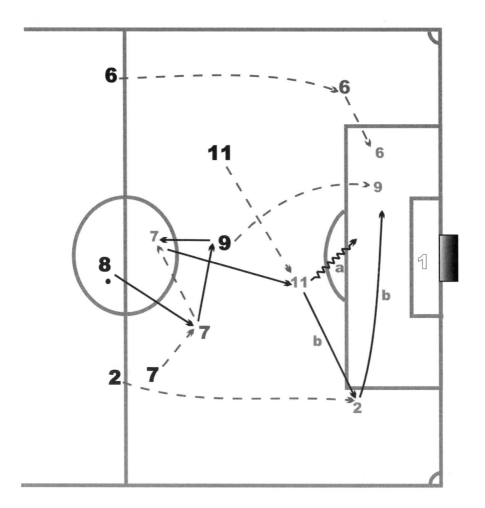

Exercises with the 4:4:2

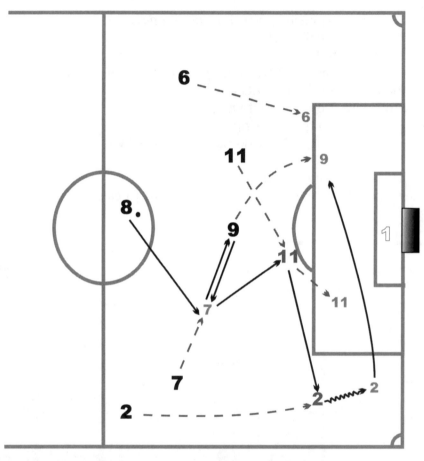

- 8 passes the ball to 7 who has come towards him;
- 7 makes a pass to 9, and gets a return pass;
- 9 and 11 criss-cross;
- 7 passes the ball to 11;
- meanwhile 2 overlaps on the wing;
- 6 cuts in towards the penalty area;
- 11 passes the ball to 2 and moves forward to get an eventual return pass;
- 2 advances with the ball for some yards and then cross-passes to 9, 6 or 11.

VARIATION
Once he has received the ball, 11 feints to pass it to 2; instead, he goes forward and shoots at goal.

Exercises with the 4:4:2

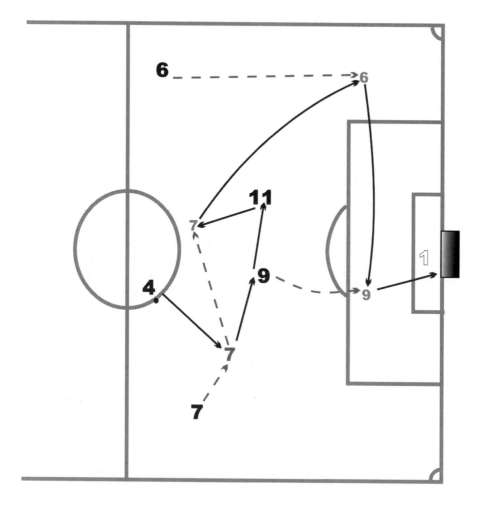

- 4 passes the ball to 7, who has come towards him to get the pass;
- 7 passes the ball to 9, who 'dummies' to let the ball reach 11 and moves into the penalty area;
- 6 gets into the left wing;
- 11 passes the ball back to 7, who has continued his movement;
- 7 makes a long pass to 6, who has got onto the left wing;
- 6 cross-passes to 9.

Exercises with the 4:4:2

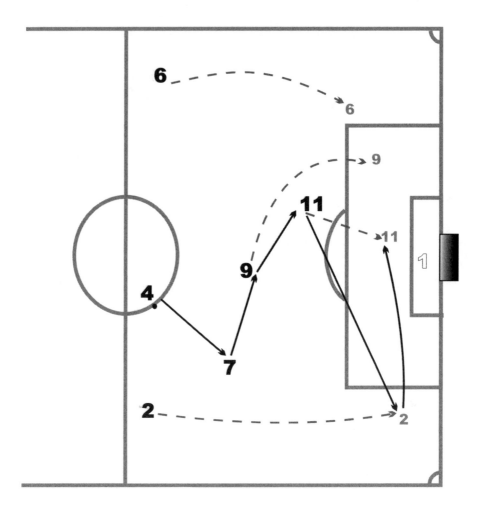

- 4 passes the ball to 7;
- 2 overlaps on the wing;
- 7 passes the ball to 9;
- 9 'dummies', lets the ball go to 11 and then overlaps him to get into the penalty area;
- 6 moves onto the left wing;
- 11 makes a long pass to 2 and moves forward to get the cross pass;
- 2 cross-passes to the center, for 9, 6 or 11.

Scheme for an Attack Started on the left, Developed on the Right Wing and Finished by a Midfielder

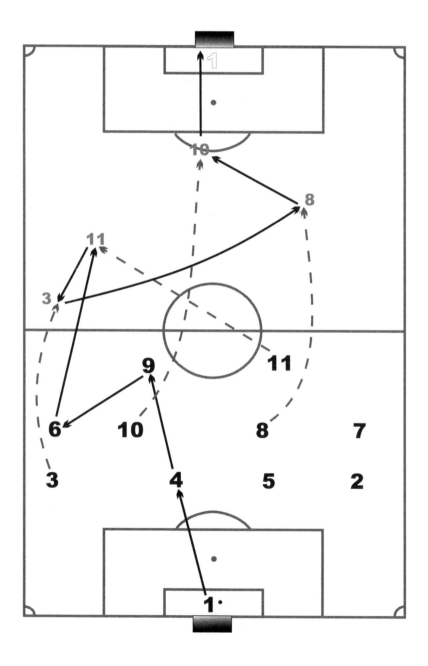

This scheme is particularly useful in a 4:4:2 arrangement.
Seven players carry out this exercise: 4, 9, 3, 11, 6, 8, 10.
The goalkeeper is the player with the ball:

- the goalkeeper passes the ball to 4;
- 4 immediately passes it to 9;
- 3 sprints along the left side line;
- 11 runs diagonally towards the left wing, overlapping 9;
- 9 passes the ball to 6;
- 6 passes it to 11;
- 8 gets into the right wing;
- 10 moves onto the center of the attack;
- 11 passes the ball to 3;
- 3 makes a long pass to 8, on the opposite side;
- 8 passes the ball to 10;
- 10 shoots at goal.

The exercise must be performed also on the right wing.

Scheme for an Attack Started on the Left and Developed on the Right Wing, with Penetration of a Midfielder and of a Linkman (or Back)

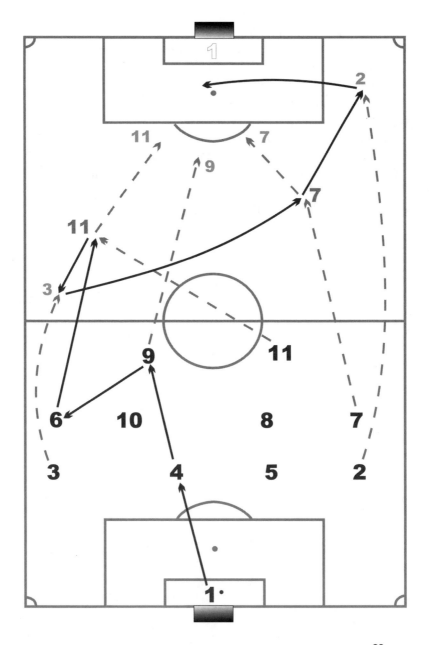

This scheme is particularly useful in a 4:4:2 arrangement.
It is a variation of the scheme which we have just dealt with.

Seven players carry out this exercise: 4, 9, 3, 11, 6, 7, 2.
The goalkeeper is the player with the ball:

- the goalkeeper passes the ball to 4;
- 4 immediately passes it to 9;
- 3 sprints along the left side line;
- 11 runs diagonally towards the left wing, overlapping 9;
- 9 passes the ball to 6;
- 7 moves quickly forward;
- 2 sprints along the right wing;
- 6 passes the ball to 11;
- 11 passes the ball to 3;
- 3 suddenly switches the play, making a long pass to 7;
- 11 and 9 follow the action going towards the goal;
- 7 passes the ball to 2;
- 2 cross-passes to the center, for 9, 7 or 11.

Scheme for an Attack Started and Developed on the Left Wing, with a Final Cross-Pass and Shot at Goal

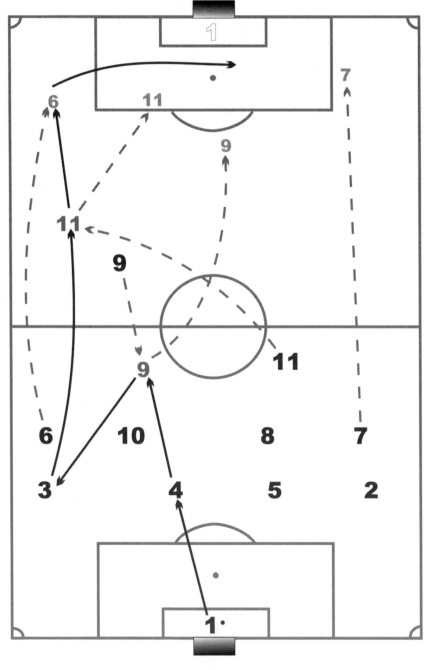

This scheme is particularly useful in a 4:4:2 arrangement.
There are the eleven players on the field, but those actively involved are 4, 9, 3, 11, 6 , 7.

The goalkeeper has the ball:
- the goalkeeper passes the ball to 4;
- 4 passes the ball to 9, who has come towards him;
- 11 sprints diagonally to the left;
- 6 starts a quick overlapping on the left wing;
- 9 passes the ball backward to 3;
- 3 makes a long pass to 11;
- 11 passes the ball to 6 and moves forward towards the goal;
- 9 follows the action;
- 7 moves onto the right wing;
- 6 cross-passes to either 9 or 11;
- 7 acts as a support or eventual alternative should the cross-pass be long.

Scheme for an Attack Started on the Left and Continued on the Right Wing Through a Cross-Pass, with Consequent Penetration of a Midfielder and Overlapping of a Side Defender

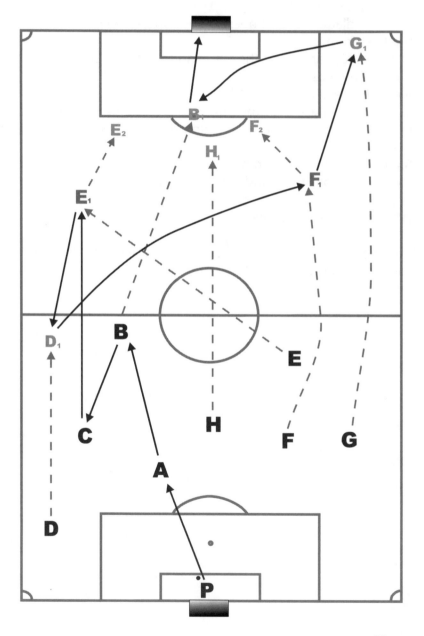

This exercise consists of switching the play, with penetration on the wing.

It is carried out by eight players, who start from positions A, B, C, D, E, F, G, H:

- the goalkeeper (P) passes the ball to A;
- A passes it immediately to B;
- B passes it backward to C;
- E cuts in diagonally and goes to position E1, where he receives the pass from C;
- D moves forward along the left wing to position D1, where he receives the pass from E;
- F runs forward to position F1;
- G quickly overlaps F on the right wing, and gets to position G1;
- D makes a cross pass to F, switching the game to the right side of the field;
- B and E move forward to positions B1 and E2;
- F passes the ball to G, and goes to position F2;
- G cross-passes to E, B or F;
- H follows the action, even if not directly involved in it.

At the moment when G cross-passes, all the players involved in the exercise are in the opponents' half of the field.

Scheme for an Attack Started on the Left and Continued on the Right Wing Through a Cross-Pass, with a Shot at Goal by a Midfielder After he has moved into the Center of the Attack

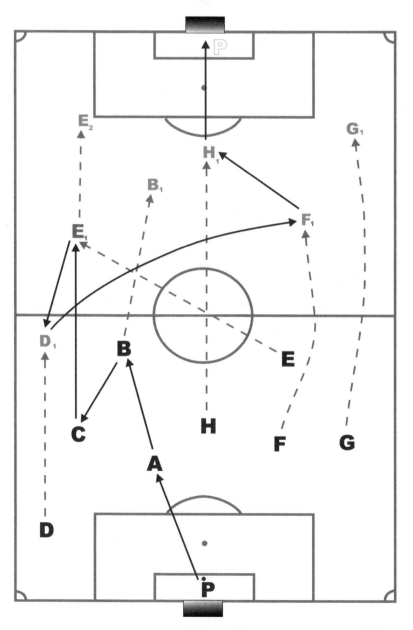

This exercise consists of switching the play, with penetration in the center.
It is carried out by eight players, who start from positions A, B, C, D, E, F, G, H.
It is a variation of the previous scheme.

The sequence of passes is identical except for the last pass:
- the goalkeeper (P) passes the ball to A;
- A passes it immediately to B;
- B passes it backward to C;
- E cuts in diagonally and goes to position E1, where he receives the pass from C;
- D moves forward along the left wing to position D1, where he receives the pass from E;
- F runs forward to position F1;
- G quickly overlaps F on the right wing, and gets to position G1;
- D makes a cross pass to F, switching the play to the right side of the field;
- midfielder H gets into the attack;
- F feints a pass to G, instead he passes the ball to H who shoots at goal.

A further variation can be the active support by E and G, to which H (if appropriately marked) can pass the ball.
Otherwise H (again if appropriately marked) can make a back pass to B, who can start a new scheme or pass the ball to E into the penalty area.

Scheme for an Attack Started and Developed on the Left Wing, with a Final Cross-Pass and Shot at Goal

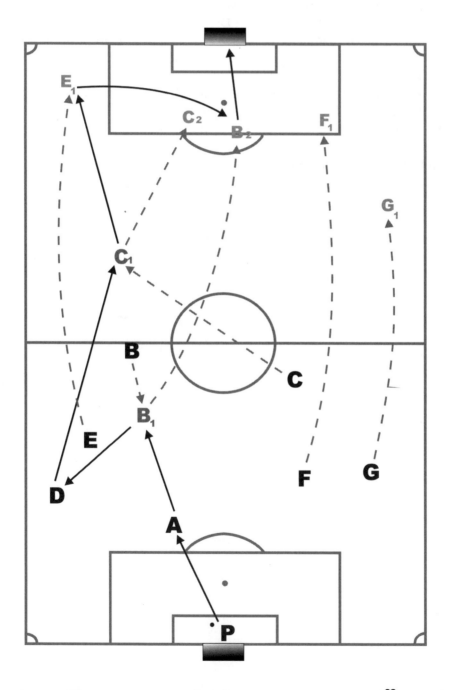

This exercise is carried out by six players who start from positions D, B, A, C, F, G:

- the goalkeeper passes the ball to A;
- A passes the ball to B, who has reached position B1;
- B passes the ball backward to D;
- C cuts across the field to receive the pass from D in position C1;
- E overlaps on the wing, reaching position E1;
- B and F run forward;
- G moves onto the wing opposite to where the action develops;
- C passes the ball to E and then goes to position C2;
- E cross-passes to the center to C, B or F.

All the players involved in the scheme have passed the midfield.

Exercise to Avoid the Off-Side Trap

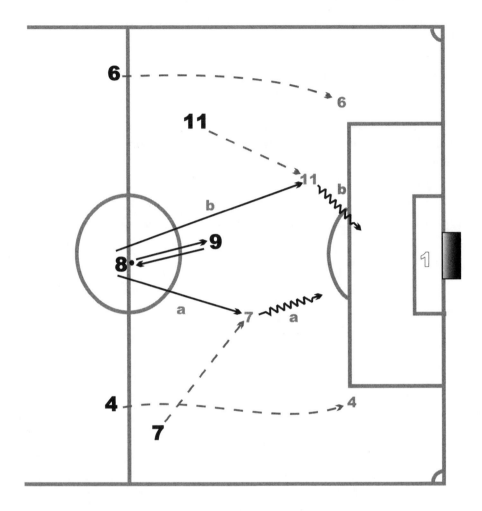

It is carried out by six players: 8, 9, 7, 4, 6, 11:

- 8 passes the ball to 9;
- 9 passes it back to 8;
- 7 and 11 cut in to receive the eventual pass;
- also 4 and 6 make a movement to receive the eventual pass from 8: they overlap on the respective wings.

If 8 manages to pass the ball to 7 (option a) or to 11 (option b) they can finish the exercise by shooting at goal.

Instead, if 8 cannot pass the ball to either 7 or 11 he can pass it to 4, who has got onto the right wing overlapping 7.
If 11 and 7 criss-cross: 11 goes to the near post and 7 goes to receive the cross-pass from 4.

Instead, if 4 makes a long cross-pass to 6, who has overlapped 11 on the left wing, 6 will cross-pass to 11.

It is important to notice that, in order to avoid the off side trap, 7 and 11 can move backward and let 4 or 6 move forward, from behind.

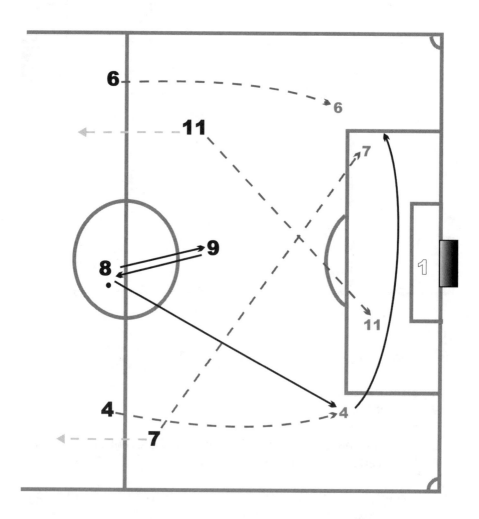

Exercise to Avoid the Off-Side Trap

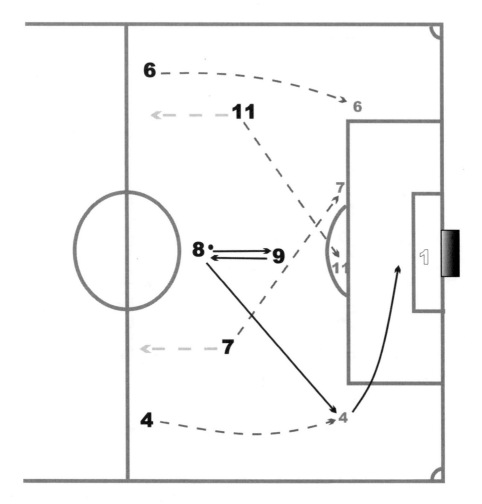

While there is a pass and a return pass between 8 and 9, the other players move as follows in order to get an eventual pass from 8:

- 4 overlaps 7 on the right wing;
- 6 moves onto the left wing;
- 7 and 11 criss-cross.

At this point 8 makes a long pass to either 4 or 6.
In order to avoid the off-side trap 7 and 11 can move backward, thus favoring the penetration of 4 and 6.
First the exercise is carried out without the backs, then with the backs applying the off-side-trap.

Exercise to Avoid the Off-Side Trap

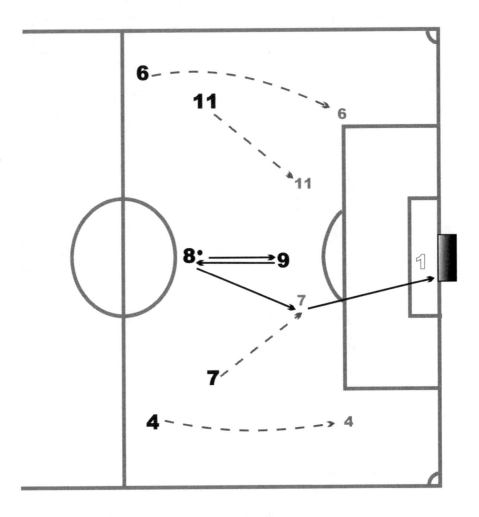

While there is a pass and a return pass between 8 and 9, the other players move as follows in order to get an eventual pass from 8:

- 7 and 11 cut in towards the center;
- 4 and 6 overlap on the respective wings.

If 8 passes the ball to 7, the latter directly shoots at goal.
Of course 8 can choose to pass the ball to 11 who can shoot at goal.

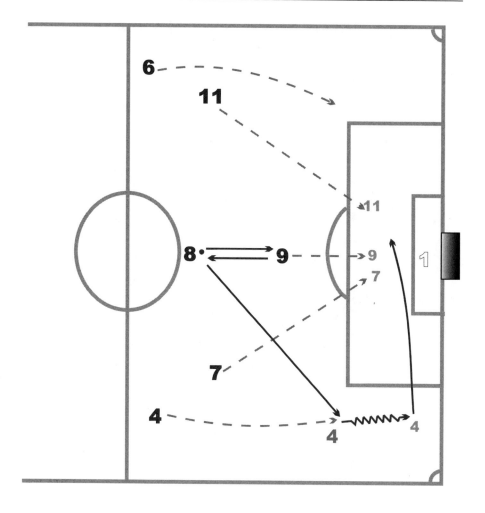

Instead, if 8 makes a long pass to 4, the latter advances with the ball towards the end of the field then cross-passes to 7, 9 or 11.

The same situation will take place on the left if 8 makes a long pass to 6.
In this exercise the choice made by 8 is very important: everything depends on him.
First the exercise is carried out without the backs, then with the backs applying the off-side trap.

Exercise to Avoid the Off-Side Trap

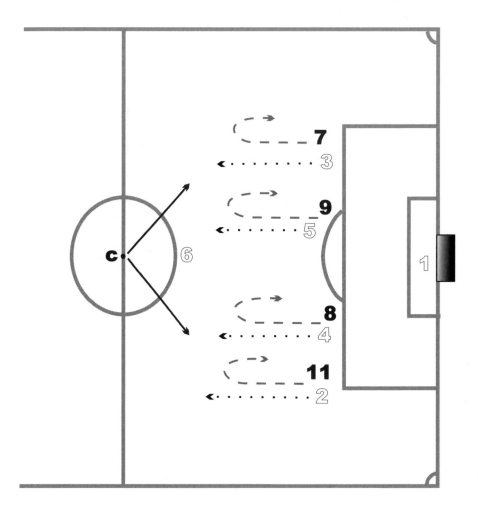

This exercise is to be carried out both by the forwards and by the attacking midfielders.

The players arrange themselves as shown in the above diagram: four forwards (7, 9, 8, 11) near the edge of the penalty area, each marked by a back (3, 5, 4, 2). In the midfield, C is the player with the ball: he is marked by 6.
The backs move forward to leave the forwards off-side.
The forwards make the same movement as the backs, but then make a quick U-turn and run towards the goal.

While moving towards the ball, each forward must be sure to keep the opposing back behind him, otherwise he will certainly be off-side when the long pass from midfielder C is made.

If we want the quick U-turn towards the goal to be really effective, it must be made almost grazing the opposing back's body (of course without committing a foul): this will prevent a quick recovery by the back.

The exercise can also be performed as follows in order to achieve good timing between the forward and the midfielder:
- the forwards are given a number (from 1 to 4);
- when the exercise starts, the midfielder shows with his hand the number of the forward he is going to pass the ball to.

The backs will be asked to turn so they cannot see the number.

Simple Exercise for the Forwards

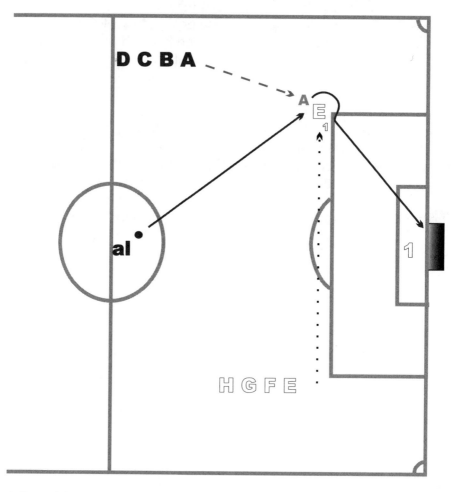

A line of forwards (D, C, B, A) and a line of backs (H, G, F, E).

The coach (al), or a player, passes the ball towards the edge of the penalty area for the penetration of the forward.

The forward tries to dribble past the back, who has gone to challenge him, in order to shoot at goal.

Of course this simple exercise can be used as a starting point for many other exercises.

Simple Exercise for the Forwards

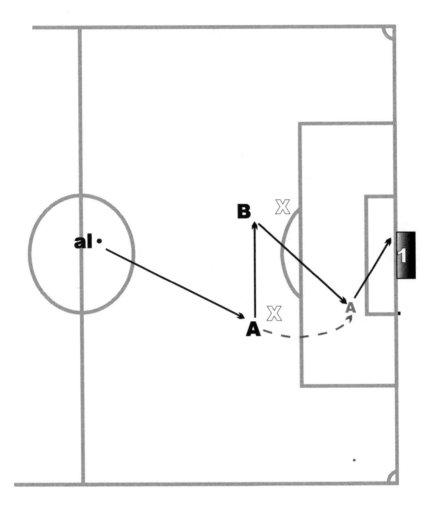

"Triangulation"

Two forwards (A and B), two backs (X and X) and the goalkeeper.

The coach (al) passes the ball to A who, pressed by the back, exchanges the ball with B in a one-touch "triangulation", then shoots at goal.

Simple Exercise for Triangulation, Overlapping, Advancing with the Ball and Shooting at Goal

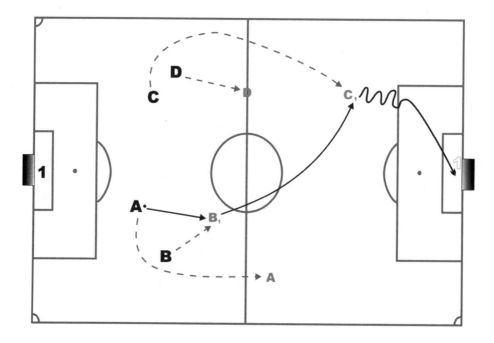

- A passes the ball to B who has moved to position B1, then over-laps on the wing;
- C overlaps D on the opposite wing and goes to position C1, where he receives the long pass from B; he advances with the ball for some yards, then shoots from the edge of the penalty area;
- D follows the action, staying behind.

First the exercise must be carried out without the backs, then with semi-active backs, finally with active backs.

It must be performed both on the right and on the left.

Double Overlapping and Shot at Goal

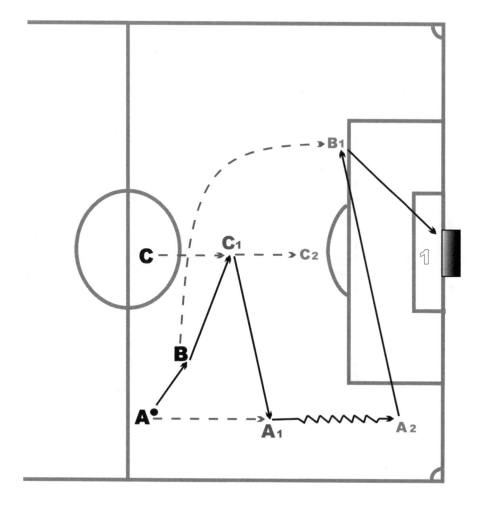

This exercise is carried out by three players: A, B, and C.

- A passes the ball to B and overlaps on the right wing;
- B passes the ball to C who has moved to position C1, then quickly overlaps to position B1;
- C passes the ball to A, who advances with the ball for a short distance and then cross-passes to B.

Later, this exercise must be carried out also with active backs.

Double Overlapping and Shot at Goal

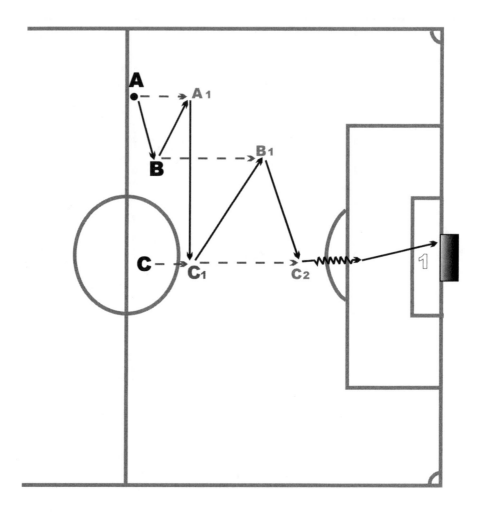

This exercise is carried out by three players: A, B, and C.

- Player A passes the ball to B and advances to get the ball back,
- he then passes it sideways to C who has moved to position C1.
- B goes to position B1 and gets the pass from C;
- C overlaps to position C2 where he receives the return pass, advances with the ball and shoots at goal.

To insist on the overlapping movement, we can tell player A to get onto the left wing in order to get a pass from C and maybe make a pass back to him.

Exercise in the Attack with Penetration of a Back and Criss-Crossing Between Midfielders

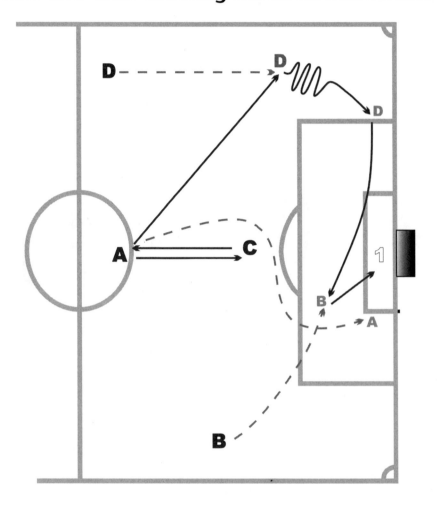

In this exercise we have a side-back (D), a midfielder (C) and two forwards (A and B):

- pass and return pass between A and C;
- quick penetration of D;
- A makes a "one-touch" pass to D and runs into the penalty area, criss-crossing with B;
- D advances with the ball up to the end of the field, then cross-passes to either A or B who shoots at goal.

Attack Exercise Aimed at Better Exploiting the Wings

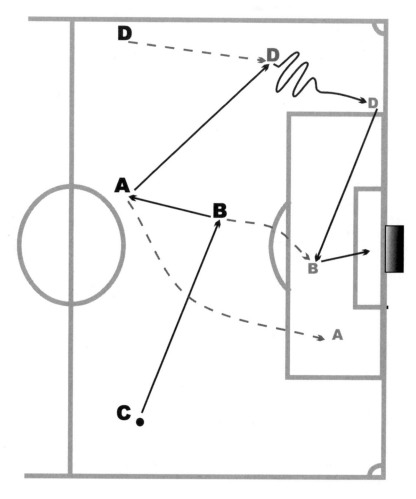

- C passes the ball to B;
- D moves onto the wing opposite to C;
- B passes the ball to A and then moves into the center of the penalty area;
- A makes a long pass to D and moves forward to support B;
- D cross-passes to either B or A.

Screen on the Side-Back by the Forward

Two forwards (9 and 11) and two midfielders (8 and 7) play against three backs (2, 5, 6):

- 7 makes a misleading movement, moving onto the right wing: thus he confuses sweeper 6, provides teammate 8 with a different option and widens the attacking front;
- 9 goes to make a screen on 2, drawing defender 5 behind him;
- 11 criss-crosses with 9 and receives a long pass from 8, then shoots at goal.

VARIATION
If forward 9 perceives that 11 has left behind his marking opponent (2), he can opt for screening sweeper 6 as the only eventual obstacle to the final action by 11.

Screen in the Attack to Prevent Territorial Marking in Outside Overlaps

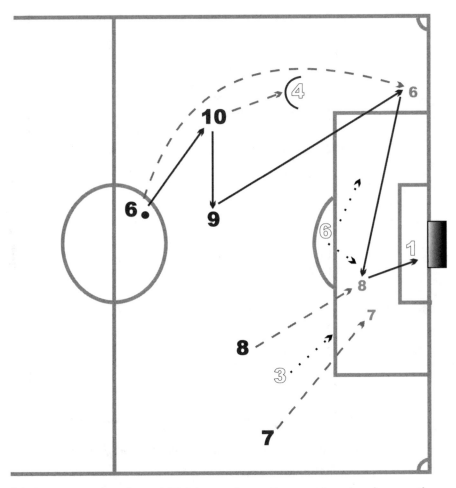

This is a screen by the midfielder to favor the overlapping by another midfielder.

Five attacking players (6, 7, 8, 9, 10) play against three defenders (3, 4 and sweeper 6):

- 6 passes the ball to 10 and overlaps on the left wing;
- 10 passes the ball sideways to 9 and makes an outside screen on defender 4 to prevent him from challenging 6;
- 9 makes a cross pass to 6;
- 8 and 9 cut into the penalty area;
- 6 cross-passes to either 8 or 7.

Screens to Prevent Territorial Marking and Marking Changes in the Outside Overlaps

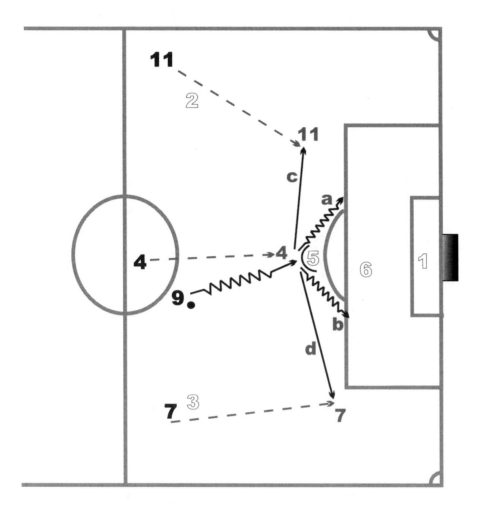

Screen by a midfielder advancing from behind the attack in order to set free a forward.

Four attacking players (11, 4, 9,7) versus four backs (2, 5, 6, 3):
- 9 advances with the ball and goes towards stopper 5;
- 4, moving forward from behind the attack, goes to screen 5, preventing or slowing down his action;
- 9 has four options, he can:
  a/b - dribble past 5 going to the right or to the left;
  c/d - pass the ball to either 11 or 7.

Screens to Prevent Territorial Marking and Marking Changes in the Outside Overlaps and in the Criss-Crossings

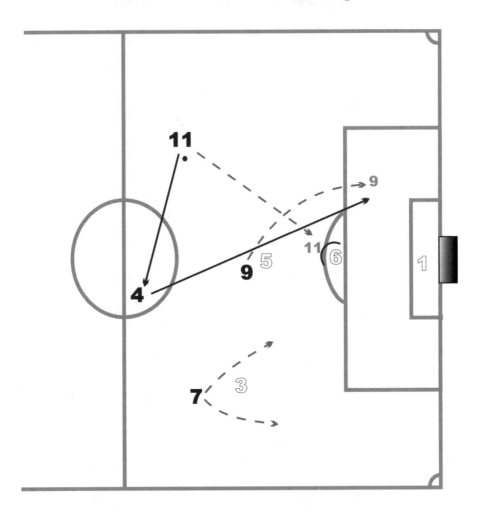

Screen on the sweeper by the forward, and criss-crossing.

Four attacking players (11, 4, 9, 7) play against three backs (6, 5, 3). 11 is the player with the ball:

- 11 passes the ball to 4, then goes to screen back 6, releasing 9;
- 9 must criss-cross with 11, trying to leave behind stopper 5;
- 4 makes a long pass to 9 who can shoot at goal;
- 7 can run into the opposite side or cut in towards the penalty area.

VARIATION

If, after getting the ball, 4 sees that the screen and the criss-crossing between 9 and 11 have failed, he can pass the ball to 7:

- on the wing, if 7 has exceeded back 3 in speed (option a);
- on the inside, if 7 has left back 3 behind (option b);
- as a support either to start the same scheme again or a new one, if 7 comes back to get the pass (option c).

To carry out the same exercise in a 4 versus 4 situation, we can add another back marking forward 11.

Later, in order to make the exercise more complex and to have more options in the attack, we can add side back 2 to the four attacking players.

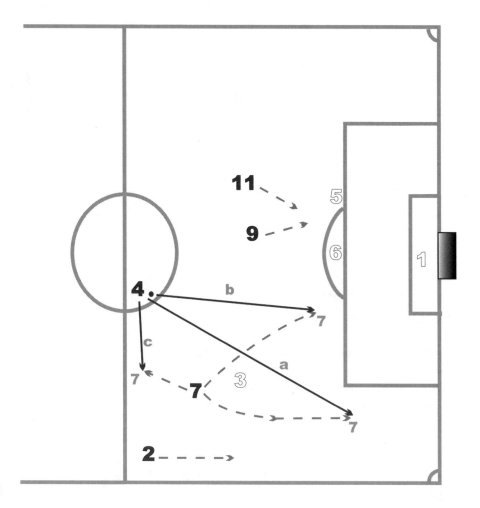

Screens to Prevent Territorial Marking and Marking Changes in the Outside Overlaps and in the Criss-Crossings

Screen by the two central forwards.

Five attacking players (11, 4, 9, 8, 7) versus 5 backs (2, 5, 6, 4, 3).
4 has the ball:

- 9 goes to screen back 4, releasing 8 who runs forward into the penalty area;
- 4 passes the ball to 8;
- 11 and 7 follow the action.

The contrary can take place too: when 4 has the ball, 8 goes to screen stopper 5, releasing 9.

Screens to Prevent Territorial Marking and Marking Changes in the Outside Overlaps and in the Criss-Crossings

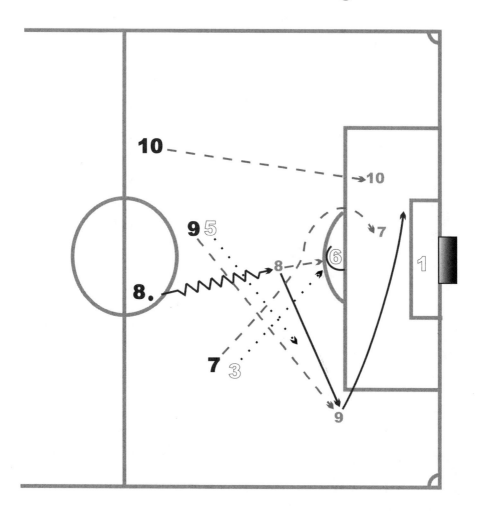

Criss-crossing of the forwards and screen by the midfielder.

Four forwards (10, 9, 8, 7) and three backs (6, 5, 3):

- 8 advances with the ball and goes towards sweeper 6;
- 7 and 9 criss-cross quickly;
- 10 moves onto the opposite wing;
- 8 passes the ball to 9 and goes to screen 6;
- 9 cross-passes to either 7 or 10.

Screens to Prevent Territorial Marking and Marking Changes in the Outside Overlaps and in the Criss-Crossings

Screen of the side back by the forward, to allow the penetration of the other forward.

Four attacking players (11, 4, 9, 7) versus four backs (2, 6, 5, 3).

4 is the player with the ball: he must make a long pass to 11.

Let's see how the other forwards move to enable 10 to receive the ball in a free position:

- 9 goes to screen back 2 to favor 11, taking with him back 5;
- 7 makes a 'dummy' movement, getting onto the opposite wing; by doing so, he:
    - a. obliges the back 3 to follow him;
    - b. alarms sweeper 6;
    - c. widens the front of the attack;
- 4 makes a long pass to 11.

At this point, wide spaces have been created in the center of the attack, with the backs confused.

In fact:
- back 6 must worry about 11 who is going towards him, and about 4 who is moving into the center of the attack;
- back 3 must worry both about 7 (who can get the pass from 11 in depth) and about 4 who is moving into the center of the attack.

Therefore, 11 must take into account the reaction of the backs; he can:
- a. try to dribble past back 6 directly;
- b. pass the ball to 4, who has come forward;
- c. make a long pass to 7.

N.B. If back 5 does not follow 9, but stays behind to help his team-mate 3, then there will be superiority in numbers on the left (9 and 11 versus 2).

Double Screen

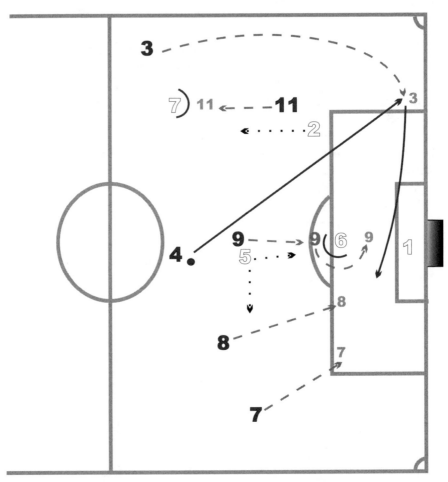

Six attacking players (3, 11, 9, 4, 8, 2) versus four defenders (7, 2, 5, 6).

4 is the player with the ball:
- 11 goes to screen 7, releasing his teammate 3 who quickly overlaps on the left wing;
- instead, 9 goes to screen sweeper 6, allowing the penetration (in the center and on the right) of 8 and 7;
- 4 makes a long pass in deep to 3;
- 3 cross-passes to either 8 or 7;
- even 9 could receive the ball if his marking opponent 5 breaks away from him (after he has seen the screen made on sweeper 6) to try to close in on 8 or 7.

Double Screen

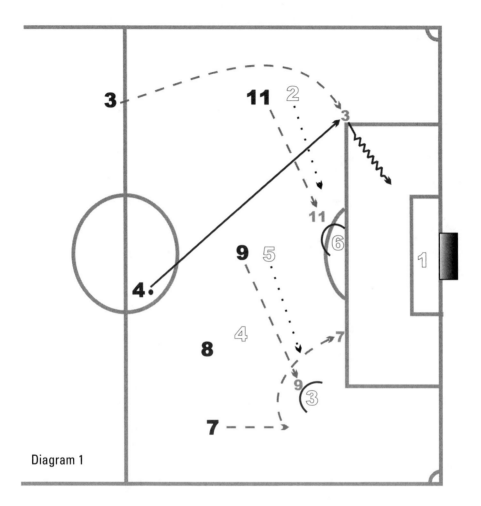

Diagram 1

Five attacking players (3, 11, 4, 9, 7) versus five backs (6, 3, 5, 4, 2).

4 has the ball.
The first option (see Diagram 1) is a direct pass from 4 to 3, who moves onto the wing, while:
- 11 goes to screen defender 6, favoring the penetration of 3;
- 9 goes to screen defender 3 favoring 7, taking back 5 with him.

We can stop here, as we are already in a position to anticipate some attacking options, shown in Diagrams 1, 2, 3 and 4.
   a. All the movements we have just described succeed: then
      3 goes directly towards the goal (see Diagram 1).

b. Back 3 somehow manages to elude the screen and to close in on 3; then 3 cross-passes to 7 (see Diagram 2).

c. instead, if back 2 closes in on 3, then 3 passes the ball to 11 who tries to dribble directly past back 6 (option a) or tries to pass the ball to 7 (option b) (see Diagram 3).

These are just examples to focus your attention on possible alternatives. Of course there can be others, always depending on the reaction and the movement of the backs.

FIRST VARIATION
Instead of going to screen 7, 9 goes to screen 4 releasing 8, who moves into the penalty area and can receive the pass from 3.

SECOND VARIATION
Carry out the exercise on the left, giving player 2 the tasks of player 3.

Diagram 2

Diagram 3

Diagram 4

Double Screen

Six attacking players (3, 11, 4, 9, 8, 7) versus four defenders (7, 2, 6, 5).

Again, the aim is to set free the side defender so that he can receive the pass from 4:
- 11 goes to screen 7, releasing 3, trying to take back 2 with him;
- 9 goes to screen sweeper 6.

In this way, 3 can either:
   a. directly move into the penalty area and shoot
   b. cross-pass to either 8 or 7.

Double Screen

Five attacking players (11, 4, 9, 7, 2) versus four backs (2, 6, 5, 3).

The aim is to create a double opportunity for midfielder 4, enabling him to either:
   a. pass the ball to 9, taking advantage of the screen on back 5 by 11;
   b. pass the ball to 2 (who has quickly moved onto the wing), taking advantage of the screen on sweeper 6 by 7.

Double Screen

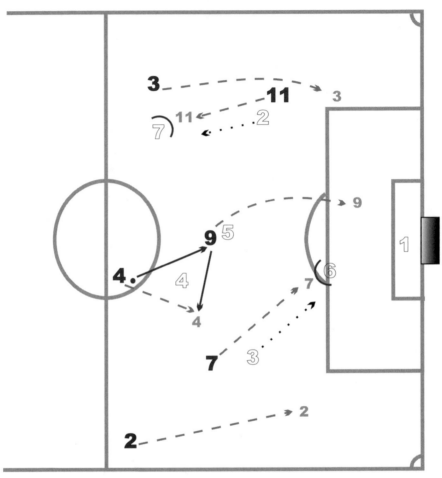

Six attacking players (11, 3, 9, 4, 7, 2) versus six defenders (2, 7, 6, 5, 4, 3).

Again, the aim is to create a double opportunity for midfielder 4: to pass the ball to 3 or to 2.

This time the scheme is quite complex, though it may turn out to be a major surprise:
- first there is a pass and a return pass between 4 and 9;
- 11 goes to screen back 7, favoring 3;
- 7 goes to screen sweeper 6, favoring 2;
- 3 and 2 overlap quickly on their respective wings;
- 9 tries to leave behind stopper 5, going to receive the eventual cross pass from 2 or 3.

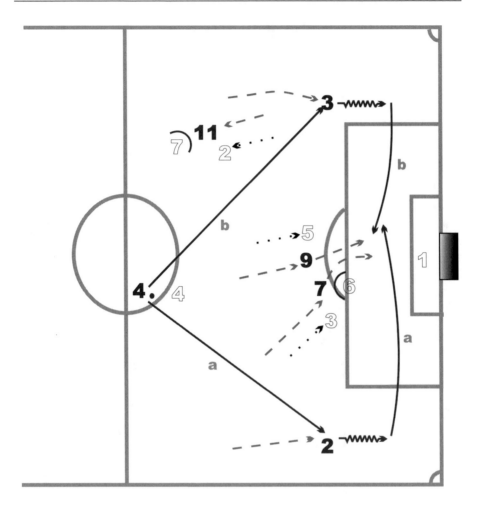

Now (see diagram above) it is easy to see option a) or option b) depending on the pass from 4.

Double Screen

Six attacking players (3, 11, 9, 4, 7, 2) versus six defenders (7, 2, 5, 4, 6, 3).

The exercise starts with an exchange in triangulation between 4 and 9.

At this point it may happen that:
    a. 2 overlaps 7 on the right wing
    b. 7 goes to screen sweeper 6, taking back 3 with him.
    c. 9 moves into the center of the attack

Then:
4 makes a pass to 2, who advances with the ball towards the end of the field, then cross-passes to 9, who must have managed to leave stopper 5 behind.

Or it may happen that (see Diagram above):

a. 11 goes to screen 7 taking with him his marking opponent 2, releasing 3 who quickly moves onto the left wing;
b. 9 moves into the center of the attack.

Then:
4 makes a long pass to 3, who cross-passes to 9.

EXERCISE FOR PRESSURE IN THE ATTACK PHASE, TAKING ADVANTAGE OF THE SUPERIORITY IN NUMBERS

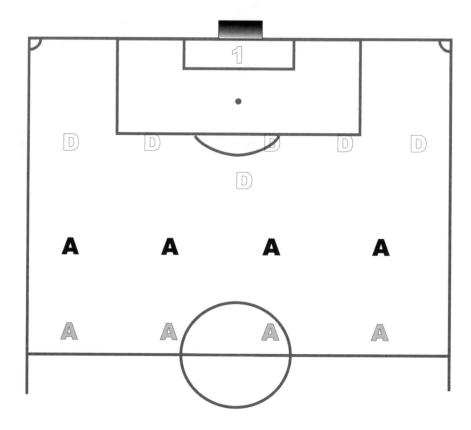

A five minute match is played on one half of the field, with only one regulation-size goal and a goalkeeper.

Team D (made up of six players) has the ball; it tries to keep possession of the ball against team A (made up of eight players), which must try to intercept the ball and start a quick attack with a shot at goal.

After five minutes (whether team A has shot at goal or not) the roles are changed. Of course, team A must "lend" two players to team D.

VARIATION

Three of the six defending players wear red shirts and three wear white shirts.

Four of the eight attacking players wear green shirts and four wear yellow shirts.

While trying to maintain the possession of the ball, a defender in red can pass the ball only to a defender in the same color. The same rule applies to a defender in white and to the attacking players when they start the attack after intercepting the ball.

Exercise for Possession of the Ball

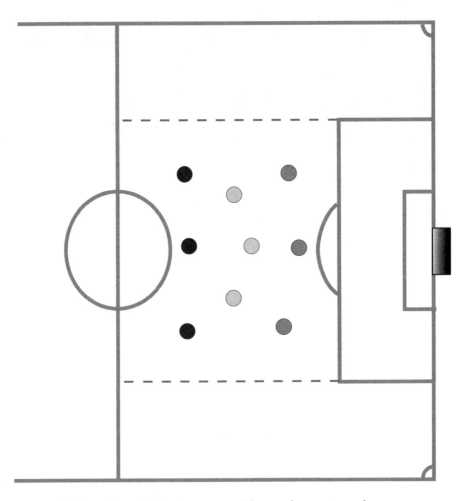

It is carried out in a limited space, with no shots at goal.

There are nine players: three in blue shirts, three in red, and three in yellow.

The exercise starts with the red and the yellow teams (6 players) versus the blue (3).

The player who makes a mistake in passing the ball forces his team to play alone against the other two. For example, if a player in red makes a mistake in passing the ball, blue and yellow will play together against red.

Of course we can add some rules to make the exercise more complex:
- restrict the number of touches (1, 2, or 3) allowed to play the ball;
- restrict the foot allowed to kick the ball (only the right or the left);
- establish that the players of the two teams playing together can pass the ball to one another only alternately: that is from a player in yellow to one in red, from one in red only to one in yellow, and so on;
- at a signal from the coach (a whistle) the supporting team changes (for example, let's imagine that the red is playing with yellow: if the signal comes when a yellow player has the ball, he will have to pass it to a blue player).

Later we can allow a shot at goal: if the shot at goal by a player is unsuccessful (either wide or saved by the goalkeeper or gone for a corner) the team to which he belongs becomes the defending team. Also, if a player loses possession of the ball before shooting at goal his team becomes the defending one.
If the shot at goal is successful, the teams do not change their roles.

As you can see, this exercise is:
- technical: various ways of kicking the ball and various touches of the ball;
- tactical: it gets the players used to attacking the opponents in three, never alone;
- physical: high pace.

Exercise for Possession of the Ball

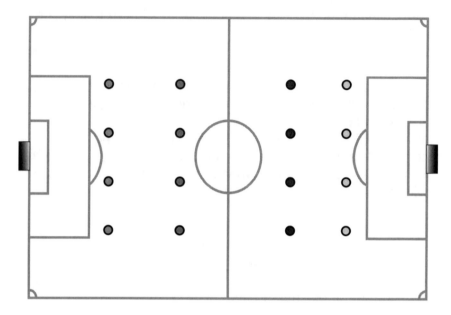

This can be carried out on a regular or smaller field.

Game with four teams (yellow, red, blue, green), each made up of three to six players (in the above example, the teams are made up of four players each).

The goalkeepers can play only on the regular field; if the exercise is carried out on a smaller field, there will be smaller goals without goal-keepers.

The length and the intervals of the exercise are fixed by the coach each time, depending on the aim.

The game starts with the red and yellow teams with the ball: they play against the blue and green teams.

The ball is actually played only by the yellow team against the green one; the red and the blue teams must only move without the ball, as if they were effectively taking part in the action. In other words:

- the red players, teammates of the attacking team, will screen the opponents or will move to receive a pass;
- the blue players, teammates of the defending team, will move "defensively" according to the position of the ball and to the movement of the red players.

That is, both teams must be ready to actively take part in the action. In fact, at a signal from the coach the red players (attacking) and the blue ones (defending) will become active players in all respects.

Physical, Technical and Tactical Exercise

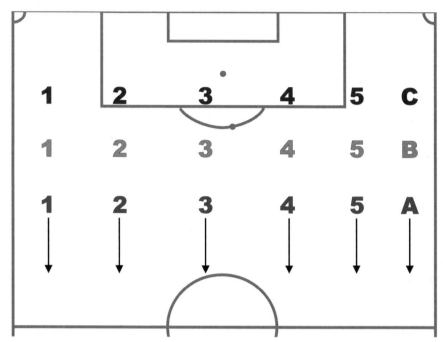

On a regular field.
The players are arranged in three lines, as shown in the above diagram.
Each player has a ball.
1. The players in line A must keep the same pace up and down the field for 3 to 7 minutes, and must all remain along the same line. Lines B and C do the same thing, keeping their distance. The pace will gradually increase.
2. The players of another line must mimic the players of the line ahead of them: the players in line A advance playing the ball with the left foot, so do the players in lines B and C.
3. The players of another line must not mimic the players of the line ahead of them, they must do the opposite: if the players in line A advance playing the ball with the left foot, the players in lines B and C will advance playing the ball with the right.
Each line will act as leading line, in turn, with a "head of line" who will also change.
For example, in the above diagram the task of "head of line" could be given to player 3 in line A, which is the leading line.
The "head of line" changes the technical performance choosing from a range previously fixed by the coach.

Physical, Technical and Tactical Exercise (Rugby)

There are three groups (A, B, C) of five players each.
The main tactical aim is to look for the "break through" and then to pass the ball sideways:
Group B starts:
- 1 advances with the ball for a short distance, then passes the ball sideways to 2 and follows the action along his own "lane";
- 2 advances with the ball, passes it sideways to 3, follows the action along his own "lane" and so on up to 4;
- 4 advances with the ball, passes it sideways to 5, overlaps, gets the pass from 5 and cross-passes;
- 1, 2 and 3 move to receive the cross-pass. So does 5, who has cut in (after his pass to 4) and occupied player 4's "lane".

Then group C starts and finally group A.

We can improve the skills, making the players kick the ball in a specific way (for example, team A can kick the ball only with one touch and with the outside of the foot, team B only with the inside and so on) or making them carry out a specific technical performance (stop and go, stop with one foot and advancing with the ball with the other, etc.).

The systematic aspect of the exercise will be taken care of through the intensity of performance that we will require of the players.

At first the exercise will be carried out without the backs; then with passive and finally with active backs.
For example, upon the cross-pass from player 4 of team B, players 1, 2, 3 of team C can defend respectively players 1, 2, 3 of team B.

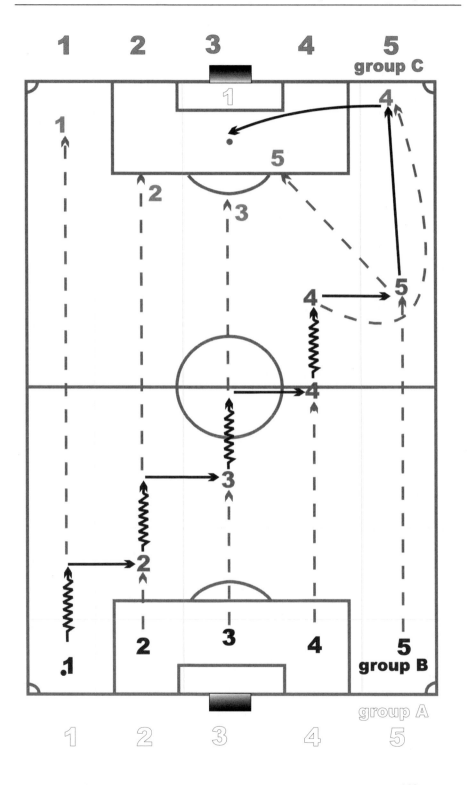

Romedio Scaia

Physical Conditioning Training for Soccer

Introduction

In our previous book, we dealt with the physical conditioning of soccer players. After ten years of new experiences we think we can give more exact advice on the coaching methods for the physical conditioning of soccer players.

After a day's study it is not so easy to start a new mental and physical involvement. Moreover, tiredness prevents the mental ability necessary to make the coaching session fruitful. So, the coach should not keep the players on the field longer than needed: it is useless to nag the players with long tactical exercises (the players' attention does not last long) or to make long theoretical speeches (maybe in the cold) when the work should instead be concentrated on clear-cut phases, with as little idle time as possible.

And if we require willingness in our players we should be the first to be always willing, even if we are a little angry or worried because of the circumstances.

Involvement and concentration do not get on well with tension: we should relieve it as soon as we realize that it is about to take the upper hand: a joke, or what we can call "the right word at the right time", is often enough to recover well-being and concentration.

In this case, the role of the coach is extremely important: as soon as he perceives tension or boredom he must immediately change the form of the exercises, without changing the "content" of the specific coaching session. A coaching session can be brought to an end earlier than expected, or a single player can be sent to the changing room, if this is a lesser evil than exercising unwillingly.

Beyond the specific knowledge, there are two important characteristics that the coach must have: level-headedness and common sense.

One example can be the coaching of the goalkeepers when, unfortunately, there is no specific partner. In this case, the goalkeepers will be required to exercise with the other players. In the first part of the session, they usually work on their own. Of course, in previous occasions we must have taught them a series of exercises that they can perform by themselves, and if one of them is older and more experienced we can give him the task to oversee the goalkeepers' specific coaching. Instead, when there is only one goalkeeper it is better to coach him with the other players, trying to finish the exercises with shots at goal and finishing the practice with a game.

Pre-Season Training Program

It should be started about one month before the beginning of the season; the ideal would be two coaching sessions a day, but this is quite rare: usually, we hold one session a day in the first two weeks, with the seventh day off. In the third week the coaching sessions become five, then they become four in the last week. After this first month, the sessions are regularly held three times a week.

In the following pages we are going to deal with the more difficult situation: pre-season sessions held once a day.

N.B. If you can hold two sessions a day, we advise you to carry out physical exercises in the morning and technical-tactical exercises in the afternoon.

DAILY WORK PLAN

The following program, and in particular the length of the exercises, is not compulsive and so should not be carried out to the letter: it is intended to give a method for operating, leaving each coach free to adjust it to his own needs and to the various circumstances.

FIRST DAY
- 20 mins. - slow run
- 10 mins. - stretching exercises
- 15 mins. - exercises for abdominal and dorsal muscles
- 30 mins. - individual skills (if possible, with a rubber ball, like the ones used in calisthenics)

SECOND DAY
- 10 mins. - general warm-up exercises
- 20 mins. - muscle exercise circuit with normal loads (see "Exercise 1")
- 25 mins. - run on slight upward slopes, at the speed of about 2.5 to 3 miles per hour
- 20 mins. - skills in pairs with rubber balls
- 10 mins. - game using only the hands on half of the field - goal to be scored by header
- 10 mins. - match using only three touches on half of the field
- 10 mins. - match using only two touches on half of the field
- 10 mins. - match on half of the field, kicking the ball only with the left foot
- 10 mins. - match on half of the field, kicking the ball only with the right foot

THIRD DAY
- 10 mins. - general warm-up exercises
- 20 mins. - muscle exercise circuit to strengthen the legs, with overload (see "Exercise 2")
- 30 mins. - run on sloping ground
- 10 mins. - stretching exercises
- 20 mins. - skills in threes with rubber balls
- 10 mins. - match using only three touches on half of the field
- 10 mins. - match using only two touches on half of the field

FOURTH DAY
- 10 mins. - general warm-up exercises
- 20 mins. - muscle exercise circuit to strengthen the abdominal and dorsal muscles, with overload (see "Exercise 3")
- 35 mins. - run on sloping ground
- 20 mins. - individual skills with a rubber ball, while moving
- 10 mins. - possession of the ball
- 15 mins. - free match on half of the field

FIFTH DAY
- 10 mins. - general warm-up exercises
- 20 mins. - mixed muscle exercise circuit, with overload (see "Exercise 4")
- 40 mins. - run on sloping ground
- 30 mins. - three work groups into which the players are divided, on different parts of the field:
    - I.   1st group: possession of the ball in a 20x20 yard square
    - II. 2nd group: slalom among cones and shot at goal from the edge of the penalty area
    - III. 3rd group: tennis-soccer
       Each activity lasts 10 minutes.
- 15 mins. - free match on half of the field

SIXTH DAY
(If a friendly match is arranged, this program will be postponed to the eighth day)
- 10 mins. - general warm-up exercises
- 20 mins. - mixed muscle exercise circuit, with overload (see "Exercise 4")
- 45 mins. - run on sloping ground
- 20 mins. - overlappings on the wings, cross passes to the center and shot at goal (with both right and left foot)
- 20 mins. - shots at goal from different positions and in different ways

SEVENTH DAY
Rest day.

EIGHTH DAY

- 10 mins. - slow run
- 10 mins. - general warm-up exercises
- 40 mins. - series of runs: 600 yards x 2, 400 yards x 3, 200 yards x 4 (in between the series, 10 minutes of active recovery with exercises for the abdominal and dorsal muscles)
- 20 mins. - individual skills with regular ball
- 20 mins. - technical matches

NINTH DAY

- 10 mins. - general warm-up exercises
- 30 mins. - muscle exercise circuit + skills (see "Exercise 5")
- 40 mins. - series of runs: 200 yards x 4, 300 yards x 3, 600 yards x 2 (in between the series, technical exercises with the ball)
- 20 mins. - exercises on the off-side trap (clearance from the defense) and rapid counterattack after intercepting the ball

TENTH DAY

- 15 mins. - slow run
- 10 mins. - general warm-up exercises
- 40 mins. - series of runs: 400 yards x 4, 200 yards x 5, 100 yards x 6 (in between the series, exercises for the abdominal and dorsal muscles)
- 20 mins. - shots at goal, after passes in twos and/or in threes
- 20 mins. - technical-tactical matches

ELEVENTH DAY

- 10 mins. - general warm-up exercises
- 20 mins. - mixed muscle exercise circuit (see "Exercise 4")
- 30 mins. - series of runs: 200 yards x 5, 100 yards x 6, 50 yards x 7 (in between the series, exercises for individual skills)
- 20 mins. - exercises on pressure and double-teaming
- 20 mins. - tactical exercises with dead ball

TWELFTH DAY

- 15 mins. - slow run
- 20 mins. - physical exercises (see "Exercise 6")
- 25 mins. - series of runs: 100 yards x 5, 80 yards x 5, 50 yards x 5
- 20 mins. - skills in twos
- 15 mins. - free match

THIRTEENTH DAY
Rest day.

At the end of these two weeks it is advisable to continue with four coaching sessions a week.

FOURTEENTH DAY
- 10 mins. - general mixed muscle warm-up exercises
- 20 mins. - mixed muscle exercise circuit
- 15 mins. - 16 inch high hurdles
- 20 mins. - series of runs: 80 yards x 5, 50 yards x 5, 30 yards x 5
- 20 mins. - exercises with final shot at goal
- 20 mins. - one, two or three-touch matches

FIFTEENTH DAY
- 15 mins. - slow run
- 10 mins. - general warm-up exercises
- 10 mins. - skipping and kicks backward with the heels
- 10 mins. - multi-jumps
- 20 mins. - series of runs: 50 yards x 5, 30 yards x 5, 10 yards x 5 (in between the series, exercises for the abdominal and dorsal muscles)
- 20 mins. - technical exercises, in threes
- 15 mins. - match with the off-side trap

SIXTEENTH DAY
- 10 mins. - general mixed muscle warm-up exercises
- 20 mins. - mixed muscle exercise circuit
- 15 mins. - 16 inch high hurdles
- 20 mins. - series of runs: 30 yards x 5, 20 yards x 5, 10 yards x 5
- 20 mins. - shots at goal, after overlapping on the wing
- 15 mins. - technical exercises between two opposite lines of players
- 15 mins. - match without restrictions

SEVENTEENTH DAY
- 15 mins. - slow run
- 10 mins. - general warm-up exercises
- 20 mins. - physical exercises (see "Exercise 5")
- 10 mins. - skipping and kicks backward with the heels
- 10 mins. - multi-jumps
- 60 mins. - match on the whole field, mixing players and substitutes or against the J.V. team

EIGHTEENTH DAY
- 10 mins. - general mixed muscle warm up exercises
- 20 mins. - mixed muscle exercise circuit (see "Exercise 5")
- 10 mins. - game using only the hands on half of the field (goal to be scored by header)
- 10 mins. - match using only one touch on half of the field
- 10 mins. - match using only two touches on half of the field
- 10 mins. - match using only three touches on half of the field
- 20 mins. - exercises of quickness among cones + 10 yard sprints with varied starts
- 20 mins. - tactical exercises with dead ball

NINETEENTH DAY
- 10 mins. - general mixed muscle warm-up exercises
- 20 mins. - choice of mixed muscle exercise circuit
- 20 mins. - series of runs: 80 yards x 3, 50 yards x 4, 30 yards x 5 (recovery while walking back to the starting point)
- 10 mins. - slalom among cones or flags dribbling the ball
- 20 mins. - shots at goal from the edge of the penalty area after a slalom dribbling through cones or flags.
- 20 mins. - technical-tactical matches

TWENTIETH DAY
- 10 mins. - general mixed muscle warm-up exercises
- 20 mins. - mixed muscle exercise circuit
- 20 mins. - series of runs: 50 yards x 3, 30 yards x 4, 10 yards x 5 (recovery while walking back to the starting point)
- 20 mins. - tactical exercises with dead ball
- 20 mins. - matches on smaller spaces

TWENTY-FIRST DAY
- 15 mins. - slow run
- 10 mins. - general warm-up exercises
- 20 mins. - series of runs: 50 yards x 3, 30 yards x 4, 10 yards x 5, then: 10 yards x 5, 30 yards x 4, 50 yards x 3 (in between the series, exercises for the abdominal and the dorsal muscles)
- 10 mins. - skipping and kicks backward with the heels
- 10 mins. - multi-jumps
- 20 mins. - overlappings, cross passes and shot at goal
- 20 mins. - match without restrictions

At this point we must face the last week of conditioning before the beginning of the season.

We will proceed to a program that we can call "unloading", with three sessions during the seven days at our disposal.

TUESDAY
- 15 mins. - slow run
- 10 mins. - general warm-up exercises
- 15 mins. - series of runs: 30 yards x 5, 20 yards x 5, 10 yards x 5 (with complete recovery)
- 20 mins. - individual skills in twos and/or threes
- 20 mins. - shots at goal in twos and/or threes
- 20 mins. - revision of the tactical exercises already dealt with

WEDNESDAY (OR THURSDAY)
Friendly match against a weaker team or with the J.V. team, to test the team to be fielded in the first match of the season, or to remove the last doubts about the line-up.

FRIDAY
- 10 mins. - slow run and general warm-up exercises
- 10 mins. - "handball" match, with goal to be scored by a header
- 10 mins. - game with only one touch
- 10 mins. - game with only two touches
- 10 mins. - game with only three touches
- 20 mins. - exercises of quickness among cones and 10 yard sprints with varied starts (see "Exercises 15, 16, 17, 18")
- 20 mins. - situations with dead ball: revision of the exercises already dealt with.

N.B. As you may have noticed, multi-jumps and hurdles have been proposed in a very moderate way as we do not want to overload the backbone.

Multi-jumps and hurdles should therefore be used moderately, also during the season, preferably when there is no game.

Breaks in the season should give us the opportunity to work more deeply on some skills developed in the pre-season period. Of course, this will depend on the length and the period of the break; for example, if the last break of the season takes place when few matches are left, it will be useless to load the players with long distance exercises: it will be better to make them do maintenance exercises, to help them recover their physical strength.

Circuit Training and Technical-Tactical Exercises

The following are exercises for the physical conditioning, some of which have already been mentioned in the above coaching program. They can be carried out in the coaching sessions both before and during the season. We have grouped them as follows:

- MUSCLE EXERCISE CIRCUITS
- PHYSICAL EXERCISE CIRCUITS
- EXERCISES TO DEVELOP QUICKNESS
- PHYSICAL AND TECHNICAL-TACTICAL EXERCISES

Strength Training Circuits

Strength Training circuits should be repeated not only in the pre-season sessions, but once a week also during the season even if we understand that few coaches may have the opportunity to use a gym or a similar place sheltered from cold and bad weather, and without such structures it is really hard to do these exercises.

Organization

The players are divided in groups of two and there will be as many work stations as pairs.

In order to control the work more easily, it is better if we place the stations in a circle.

On the coach's whistle, one player starts to work while the other assists him (for example, by holding his ankles).

After thirty seconds' work, they change roles, and the second player does the same exercise for thirty seconds.

The break between their respective work is thirty seconds.

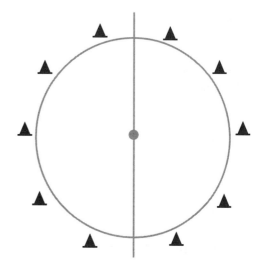

Then, the pair goes to the next station leaving their place to the pair after them.

The muscle exercise circuit must be done after a good general warm-up, before the other physical exercises.

Equipment needed:

Using the following we can have a real gym at our disposal:
- 4-pound dumbbells (four pairs)
- 8-pound medicine balls (at least four)
- wooden sticks (at least ten)
- 4-pound iron sticks (at least five)
- one 16/20-pound barbell
- two or three benches (usually, the ones in the changing room)

CIRCUIT 1
Muscle Exercise Circuit with Almost Natural Load - In Pairs

Times: 30 seconds work - 1 minute recovery
Equipment needed: dumbbells, medicine ball, wooden sticks.

- 1 - Standing up: bring the outstretched arms together in front of the body, holding the dumbbells; keeping arms straight.
- 2 - lying on the back, feet held by the partner, arms crossed on the chest: raise the upper body up to 45 degrees, then go down to the ground;
- 3 - face downward, feet held by the partner, hands on the back of the neck: tension of the dorsal muscles; bringing shoulders up as far as possible
- 4 - standing up, wooden stick on the back of the neck: rotation of the upper body to the right and to the left;
- 5 - standing up: hold the dumbbells and bend the arms behind the head;
- 6 - lying on the back, legs open wide and held by the partner: bend the upper body towards the right foot, then towards the left and so on;
- 7 - standing up, stick high over the head: sideways bending of the upper body;
- 8 - standing up, hold the dumbbells: rotate the arms forward and backward;
- 9 - lying on the back, legs open wide, medicine ball between the ankles, bend the upper body forward. Alternate with and without the ball;
- 10 - face downward, hold the medicine ball on the back of the neck: tense the dorsal muscles, bringing shoulders up as far as possible.

CIRCUIT 2
Muscle Exercise Circuit with Overload for the Legs - In Pairs

Times: 30 seconds work - 1 minute recovery
Equipment needed: barbell, medicine ball, iron sticks, 16-inch-high hurdles.

- 1 - Hold an iron stick: jump, pushing the stick up in coordination with the feet's upthrust;

- 2 - double foot jumps over six 16 inch high hurdles, placed at intervals of 1 yard, with a hop in-between;
- 3 - standing up, iron stick on the shoulders: hops on the spot with legs slightly apart;
- 4 - squat (half-bent legs) with two iron sticks on the shoulders;
- 5 - complete knee-bends with iron stick on the shoulders;
- 6 - standing up, barbell on the shoulders and heels slightly raised (about 2 inches): quick half squat;
- 7 - hops with legs wide apart, holding two iron sticks on the shoulders and pushing them up in coordination with the feet's upthrust;
- 8 - lying on the back, medicine ball between the feet: take it behind the head with outstretched legs, then back to the starting point;
- 9 - standing up, two iron sticks on the shoulders: hops forward and backward (open the legs wide forward and backward).

CIRCUIT 3
Muscle Exercise Circuit with Overload for Abdominal and Dorsal Muscles - In Pairs

Times: 30 seconds work - 1 minute recovery
Equipment needed: dumbbells, medicine ball, iron sticks.

- 1 - Lying on the back, outstretched legs held by the partner: raise and bend the upper body forward, holding the iron stick on the back of the neck;
- 2 - face downward, ankles held by the partner: tense the dorsal muscles, holding the iron stick on the back of the neck;
- 3 - lying on the back, medicine ball held on the chest: raise the upper body up to 45 degrees and keep this position for about 30 seconds;
- 4 - lying on the left side: raise the upper body holding the medicine ball over the head, then go back to the starting position;
- 5 - lying on the right side: raise the upper body holding the medicine ball over the head, then go back to the starting position;
- 6 - face downward, with medicine ball held on the back of the neck: raise and lower the upper body;
- 7 - sitting, half-bent legs held by the partner: with the iron stick on the back of the neck, tilt the upper body backward, with rotations to the right and to the left;
- 8 - face downward, legs held by the partner: raise the upper body then take the medicine ball over the head and under the

chin, alternately;

- 9 - lying on the back, legs outstretched upward towards the partner: the partner, standing up, pushes the other player's legs downward. The exercising player must put up resistance;
- 10 - lying on the back, legs wide apart and holding the dumbbells: bend the upper body forward taking the right dumbbell to the left foot and vice versa. Go back to the initial position and so on.

CIRCUIT 4
Mixed Muscle Exercise Circuit, with Overload - in Pairs

Times: 30 seconds work - 1 minute recovery
Equipment needed: dumbbells, medicine ball, barbell.

- 1 - barbell on the shoulders: squat (half-bent knees);
- 2 - barbell on the shoulders: bend the upper body down to 90 degrees and go back to the starting position;
- 3 - lying on the back, with legs on the bench and the upper body off of it, on the ground; feet held by the partner, take the medicine ball and touch it to the feet, then go back to the starting point;
- 4 - face downward, legs on the bench with the upper body off of it: with the medicine ball on the back of the neck, tense the dorsal muscles;
- 5 - standing up, legs shoulder width apart: hold the barbell (after bending the upper body forward to 90 degrees) and take it to the height of the shoulders without lifting up the upper body (only the arms work);
- 6 - lying on the back, barbell at the height of the chest: push the barbell upward, then take it back to the starting position;
- 7 - lying on the back, legs wide apart and outstretched: hold the medicine ball and take it in between the legs, bending the upper body forward;
- 8 - face downward, feet held by the partner, holding the dumbbells: bend the upper body backward, with rotations to the right and to the left;
- 9 - sideways bending to the right, holding the medicine ball over the head with arms outstretched;
- 10 - sideways bending to the left, holding the medicine ball over the head with arms outstretched.

CIRCUIT 5
Mixed Muscle Exercise Circuit and Skills

The players are divided into groups and each group is given a work station.
The exercises are carried out for 10 minutes at each station, in turn.

- **1st STATION:** double foot jumps over 6 hurdles: the hurdles are about 16 inches high and are placed at intervals of one yard;

- **2nd STATION:** exercises for the abdominal and dorsal muscles with medicine ball;

- **3rd STATION:** slalom through cones dribbling the ball, kicking it in various ways (with the outside or the inside of the foot and so on);

- **4th STATION:** sitting on the bench, outstretched arms holding the medicine ball: rotations of the upper body to the right and to the left;

- **5th STATION:** possession of the ball in a 10 yard square: 2 versus 2, 3 versus 3, 4 versus 4.

Interval Training

Physical exercise circuits

The following physical circuits (#6 to #12) allow physical conditioning while at the same time facing various game situations: long runs increasing the speed, sprints, slaloms, take-offs for headers and so on. They also allow coaching without boring repetitions and with more concentration, as the exercises appear constantly varied.

These exercises should be performed during the first session of the week after a good general warm-up.

N.B. If the coach thinks that his team needs more coaching, the following exercises can be preceded by "Exercise 13".

Finally, "Circuit 14" can be done as an alternative to the following physical circuits, but only at the beginning of the week.

CIRCUIT 6
Physical Exercise Circuit

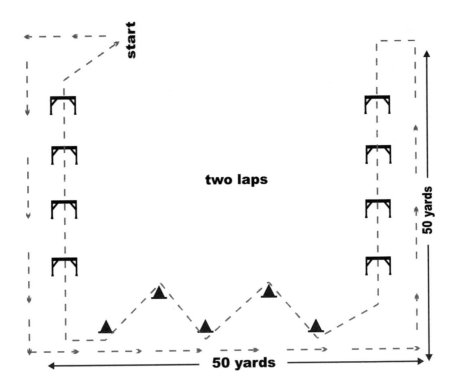

2 laps:

- double foot jumps over 16 inch high hurdles, placed at intervals of 8 yards;
- quick slalom among the cones;
- jumping taking off of one foot over 16 inch high hurdles, placed at intervals of 1 yard.

CIRCUIT 7
Physical Exercise Circuit

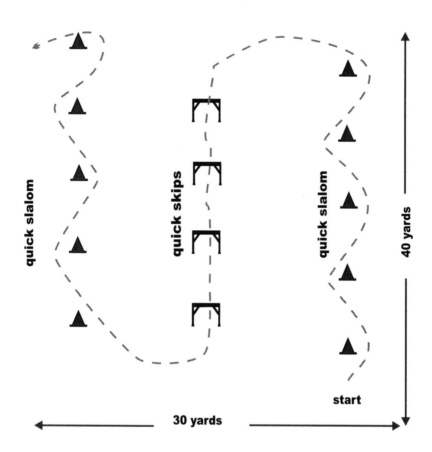

2 laps:

- quick slalom among the cones;
- double foot jumps over four 16 inch high hurdles, placed at intervals of 2 yards, with quick skips in between jumps;
- quick slalom among the cones.

CIRCUIT 8
Physical Exercise Circuit

Around the perimeter of the field.
Four laps.
Recovery in between laps: when all the players have finished a lap, the first player starts again.

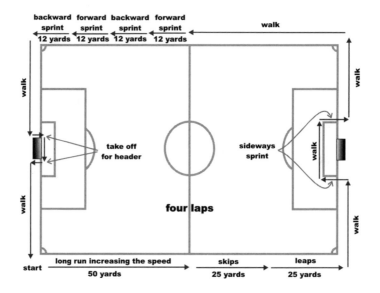

- 50 yard run increasing the speed;
- 25 yards in skips;
- 25 yards in leaps;
- walk up to the crossing between the goal line and the line of the six yard goal area;
- sideways sprint along the shorter line of the goal area;
- walk along the longer line of the goal area;
- sideways sprint along the shorter line of the goal area (on the other side);
- walk up to the midfield;
- sprint forward for 12 yards;
- sprint backward for 12 yards;
- sprint forward for 12 yards;
- sprint backward for 12 yards;
- walk up to the goal;
- take off for header on the near post;
- take off for header on the far post.

CIRCUIT 9
Physical Exercise Circuit

Around the perimeter of the field.
Five laps.
Recovery in between laps: when all the players have finished a lap, the first player starts again.

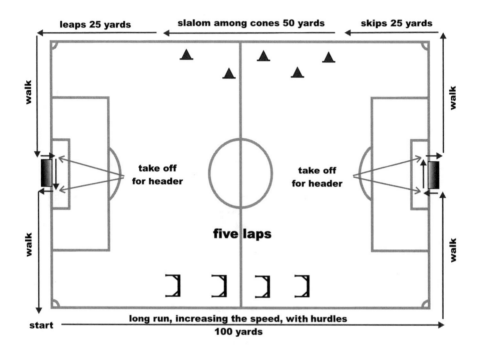

- 100 yard run increasing the speed, jumping four 16 inch high hurdles placed at intervals of 5 yards;
- walk up along the goal line;
- take off for header on the near post;
- take off for header on the far post;
- skips for 25 yards;
- slalom among cones;
- leaps for 25 yards;
- walk along the goal line;
- take off for header on the near post;
- take off for header on the far post;
- walk along the goal line.

CIRCUIT 10
Physical Exercise Circuit

Half of the field (lengthwise) is used.

Four laps.

Recovery in between laps: when all the players have finished a lap, the first player starts again.

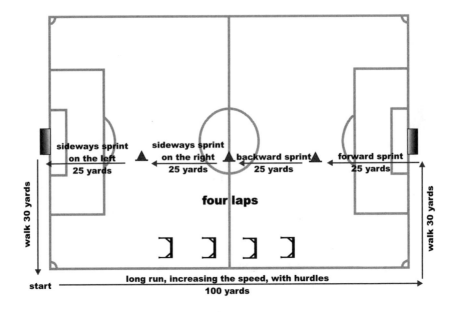

- 100 yard run increasing the speed, jumping four 16 inch high hurdles placed at intervals of 5 yards;
- walk up to the center of the goal;
- sprint forward for 25 yards;
- sprint backward for 25 yards;
- sprint sideways on the right for 25 yards;
- sprint sideways on the left for 25 yards;
- walk from the center of the goal to the starting point.

CIRCUIT 11
Physical Exercise Circuit

On a quarter of the field.

Five laps.

Recovery in between laps: when all the players have finished a lap, the first player starts again.

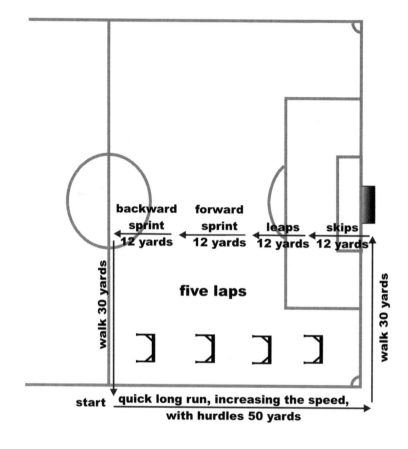

- 50 yard run increasing the speed, jumping four 16 inch high hurdles placed at intervals of 10 yards;
- walk up to the center of the goal;
- skips for 12 yards;
- leaps for 12 yards;
- sprint forward for 12 yards;
- sprint backward for 12 yards;
- walk from the midfield to the starting point.

CIRCUIT 12
Physical Exercise Circuit

On half of the field.

Five laps.

Recovery in between laps: when all the players have finished a lap, the first player starts again.

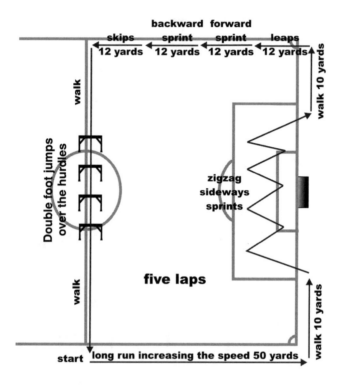

- 50 yards in quick long run increasing the speed;
- walk 10 yards;
- zigzag sideways sprint for 15 yards;
- walk 10 yards;
- leaps for 12 yards;
- sprint forward for 12 yards;
- sprint backward for 12 yards;
- skips for 12 yards;
- walk 10 yards;
- double foot jumps over the six 16 inch high hurdles placed at intervals of 1 yard;
- walk 10 yards.

CIRCUIT 13
Physical Exercise Circuit

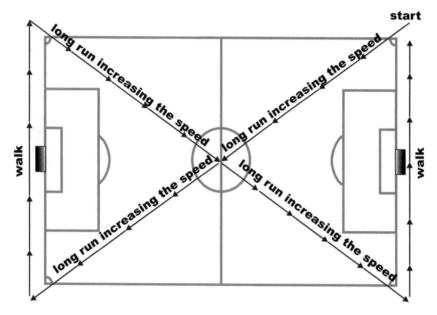

- 4 long runs increasing the speed, from corner to corner, diagonally.

- 4 quick long runs, from one corner to the midfield, diagonally.

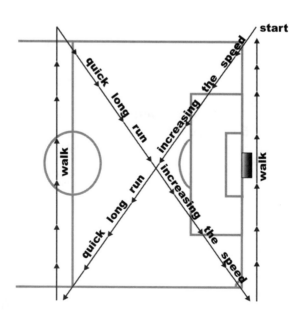

- 4 laps with sprints around the penalty area.

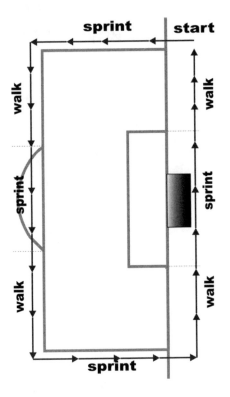

- 4 laps with sprints around the 6 yard goal area.

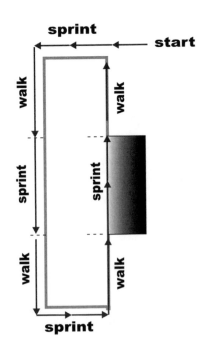

CIRCUIT 14
Physical Exercise Circuit - Changes in Speed

1st SERIES - To be repeated 10 times
- fast run (30 seconds)
- slow run (30 seconds)

2nd SERIES - To be repeated 5 times
- fast run (1 minute)
- slow run (30 seconds)
- fast run (30 seconds)
- slow run (1 minute)

3rd SERIES - To be repeated once
- fast run (1 minute)
- slow run (1 minute)
- fast run (30 seconds)
- slow run (30 seconds)
- fast run (20 seconds)
- slow run (20 seconds)
- fast run (10 seconds)
- slow run (10 seconds)
- fast run (20 seconds)
- slow run (20 seconds)
- fast run (30 seconds)
- slow run (30 seconds)
- fast run (1 minute)
- slow run (1 minute)

EXERCISES TO DEVELOP QUICKNESS

These should be carried out two days before the match.
Recovery must be complete.

CIRCUIT 15
Sprints among rubber cones - In pairs

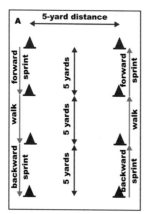
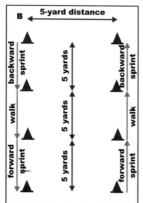
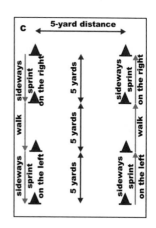

Two lines of four cones each, placed at intervals of 5 yards.
Also the distance between the two lines is about 5 yards.

First series
From the first to the second cone: forward sprint.
From the second to the third cone: walk.
From the third to the fourth cone: backward sprint.

Second series
From the first to the second cone: backward sprint.
From the second to the third cone: walk.
From the third to the fourth cone: forward sprint.

Third series
From the first to the second cone: sideways sprint on the right.
From the second to the third cone: walk.
From the third to the fourth cone: sideways sprint on the left.

CIRCUIT 16
Sprints, criss-crossings and sideways runs - In pairs

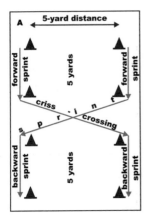 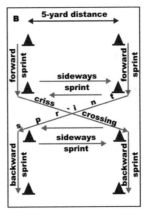 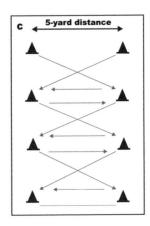

First series

From the first to the second cone: forward sprint.
From the second to the third cone: criss-crossing between the two players (while sprinting).
From the third to the fourth cone: backward sprint.

Second series

From the first to the second cone: forward sprint.
On the second cone: sideways sprint.
From the second to the third cone: criss-crossing between the two players (while sprinting).
On the third cone: sideways sprint.
From the third to the fourth cone: backward sprint.

Third series

From the first to the second cone: criss-crossing between the two players (while sprinting).
On the second cone: sideways sprint.
From the second to the third cone: criss-crossing between the two players (while sprinting).
On the third cone: sideways sprint.
From the third to the fourth cone: criss-crossing between the two players (while sprinting).
On the fourth cone: sideways sprint.

CIRCUIT 17
Zigzag sprints - One player at a time

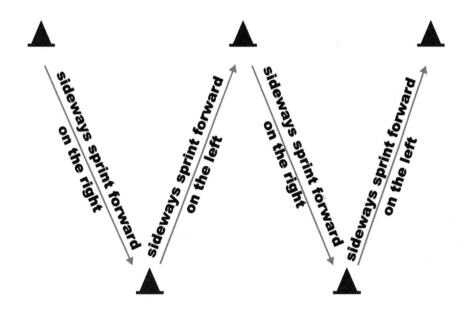

First series
From the first to the fifth cone: series of forward sprints, slowing down at every cone (see above).

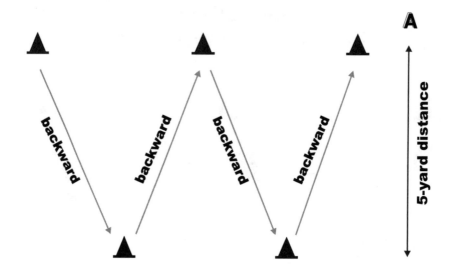

Second series

From the first to the fifth cone: series of backward sprints (see above), slowing down at every cone.

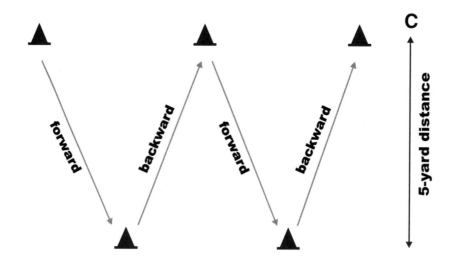

Third series

(Above) From the first to the second cone: forward sprint.
From the second to the third cone: backward sprint.
From the third to the fourth cone: forward sprint.
From the fourth to the fifth cone: backward sprint.

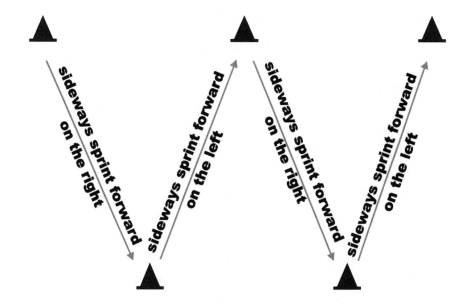

Fourth series

(Above) From the first to the second cone: sideways sprint on the right.

From the second to the third cone: sideways sprint on the left.

From the third to the fourth cone: sideways sprint on the right.

From the fourth to the fifth cone: sideways sprint on the left.

CIRCUIT 18
Sprints with varied starts (7/8 yards)

- 1 - players in front of the coach: upon the first whistle, quick skips on the spot; upon the second, forward sprint for 8 yards;

- 2 - players sitting in front of the coach: upon the whistle, stand up quickly and sprint;

- 3 - players sitting, their backs turned on the coach: upon the whistle, turn to the right and sprint towards the coach;

- 4 - lying on the back, feet towards the coach: upon the whistle, stand up quickly and sprint;

- 5 - lying on the back, head towards the coach: upon the whistle, turn to the left and sprint towards the coach;

- 6 - face downward, feet towards the coach: upon the whistle, turn on the right and sprint towards the coach;

- 7 - face downward, head towards the coach: upon the whistle, sprint towards the coach;

- 8 - knee-bend: upon the whistle, sprint towards the coach.

EXERCISE FOR SPEED AND QUICKNESS OF REFLEX

EXERCISE 19

These are 8 yard sprints, to be done both to improve quickness of reflex and to assess the psychological-physical condition of the player.

For example: put small flags of different colors on the ground. The coach calls out a color: the player must immediately sprint to the corresponding small flag.

Further example: put three balls at intervals of 8 yards, naming them "1, 2, 3" (or "New York, Chicago, Los Angeles"): the player must immediately sprint to the symbol called out by the coach.

Further example: put the player in between two small flags (one red and one yellow) placed at about 10 yards from each other. In front of the feet of the player there is the ball.

The rule is that if the coach calls out "yellow" the player must sprint to that small flag, without the ball; if the coach calls out "red" the player must advance with the ball to that small red flag.

After some times, we can ask the player to do the contrary.

TACTICAL MATCHES

To the player, the match is certainly the most interesting part of the coaching session: in fact he thinks that, after the boring and tiring phase, this is time for fun.

Unfortunately, there are some coaches who endorse this way of thinking: they start to referee wearily for about twenty minutes, without dictating the rules and without interfering: then everybody to the showers!

Instead, if we want the match to be useful we must first of all establish some rules according to the aims we want to reach through the match. Then, the coach must watch the match very carefully: this certainly motivates the players.

For example, restricting touches to two or three makes the match more serious and the players more concentrated.

Anyway, we can allow the players to play matches without restrictions once in a while.

Those who have the chance of having a regulation-size field should play these matches on one half of the field.

1. Match with 1, 2 or 3 touches.

2. Match kicking the ball only with the right foot or only with the left.

3. Match in which the goal is valid only if all the players of the scoring team have passed the midfield (this gets the players used to keeping the team short and compact).

4. Match with the off-side trap (to get the forwards used to coming back to the midfield).

5. Match in which the goal is valid only if scored after overlapping a teammate, or after a cross pass to the center, or after any overlapping on the wings.

TECHNICAL-TACTICAL AND PHYSICAL EXERCISES

1. Technical-Tactical Exercise
Shot at Goal

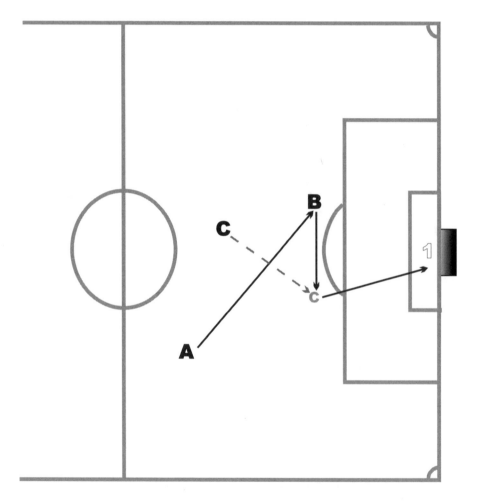

- Player A passes a middle height ball to teammate B;

- with a volley touch (foot or header) B passes the ball to C's feet, who meanwhile has come forward diagonally;

- C shoots directly at goal.

2. Technical Exercise
Shot at Goal

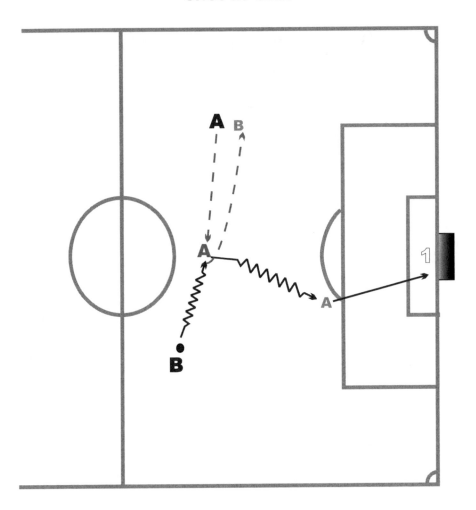

- B dribbles the ball towards A, who moves towards him and takes over the ball;

- A dribbles the ball towards the penalty area and, from the edge, shoots at goal;

- B takes A's place.

3. Technical Exercise
Shot at Goal

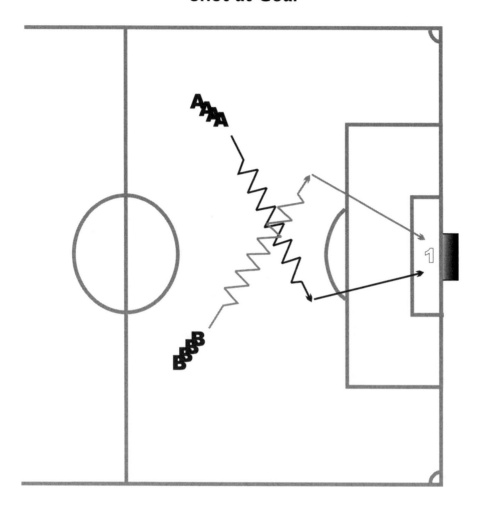

The players dribble the ball diagonally, starting from two opposite lines; they criss-cross and shoot at goal.

The players in one line dribble the ball with the instep, then shoot with the outside of the foot.

The players in the other line dribble the ball with the outside of the foot, then shoot with the instep.

4. Technical Exercise
Shot at Goal

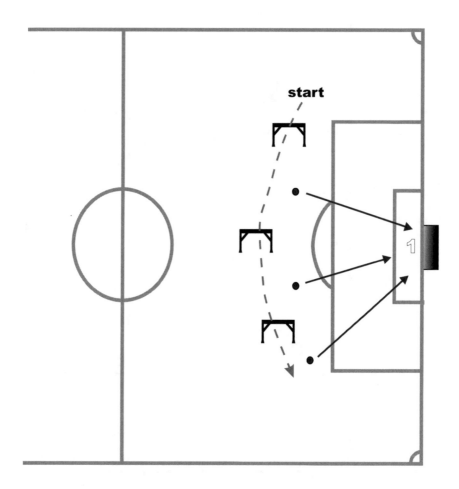

After jumping over each hurdle, the players shoot at goal.

The balls can be ready on the ground or can be passed by a teammate in good time.

If we increase the number of hurdles, the exercise becomes physical as well.

5. Technical Exercise
Pass, Stop, Shot at Goal

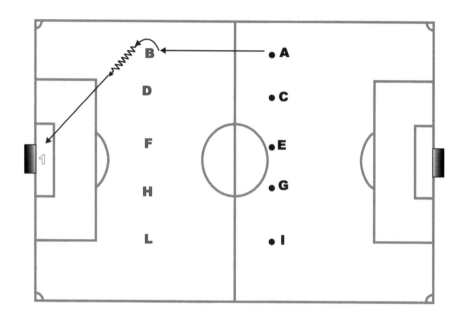

A line of players is arranged in the midfield; each player has a ball.

Some yards outside the penalty area there is another line of players, with their backs turned to the goal.

Player A passes the ball to B who controls it, turns and shoots at goal.

Both the way of kicking the ball and the way of controlling it (with the left or with the right foot, with the chest, with the head, and so on) should be made different from player to player.

The passes can be changed too: on the second go, A passes the ball to L, C to H and so on.

After some repetitions, exchange roles.

6. Physical-Technical Exercise
Double Shot at Goal and Exercise for Cross Passes

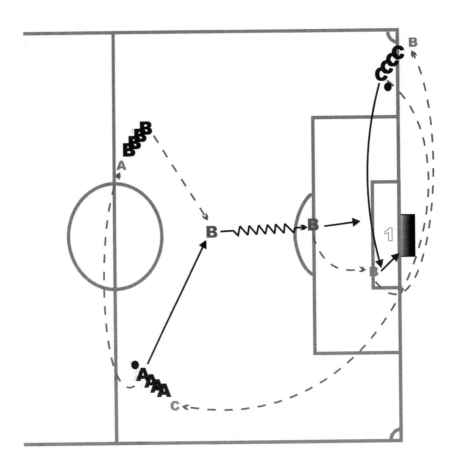

Three lines of players, arranged as shown in the above diagram.

- A passes the ball to B, who has come forward to receive the pass;

- B controls the ball, dribbles it up to the edge of the penalty area and shoots at goal. Then he keeps on running to receive the cross pass from C with a header;

- A, B and C respectively go to the end of lines B, C and A.

7. Technical-Tactical Exercise
Two-Player-Game to Shoot at Goal

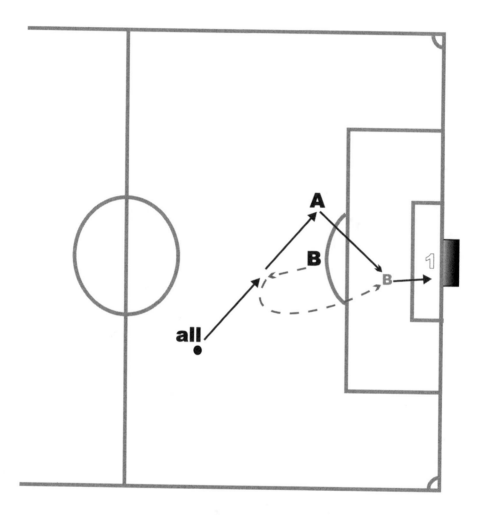

The coach (all), or another player, passes the ball to B, who comes towards him feinting to receive it; instead, he lets it go to A and moves quickly into the penalty area, where he receives the pass from A and shoots at goal.

8. Technical-Tactical Exercise
Three-Player-Game to Shoot at Goal

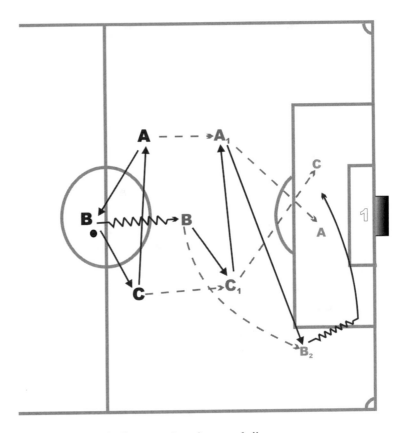

A, B and C pass the ball to each other as follows:
- B passes the ball to C;
- C passes it to A and goes to position C1;
- A passes it back to B and goes to position A1;
- B dribbles for a short distance and passes the ball to C1; then moves onto the wing to position B2;
- C1 passes the ball to A1 and moves quickly into the penalty area;
- A1 makes a long pass to B2 and moves into the penalty area, criss-crossing with C;
- B2 advances towards the goal line, then cross-passes to A and/or C.

The exercise must also be done on the left and the players must take turns in the different positions.

9. First Variation to Exercise 8

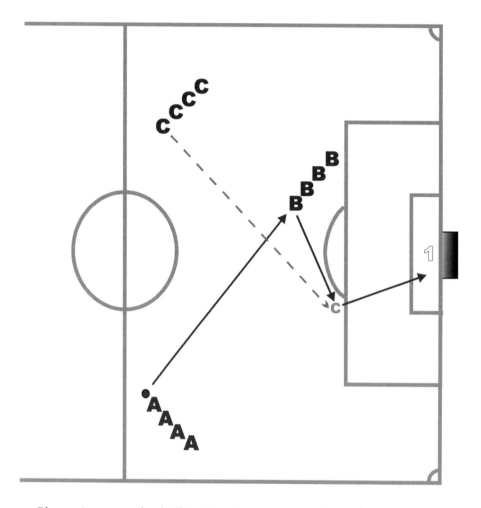

- Player A passes the ball to B, who passes on the volley to C, who has moved diagonally forward in good time;

- C shoots at goal.

Repeat the exercise also on the left; the players must take turns in the different positions.

10. Second Variation to Exercise 8

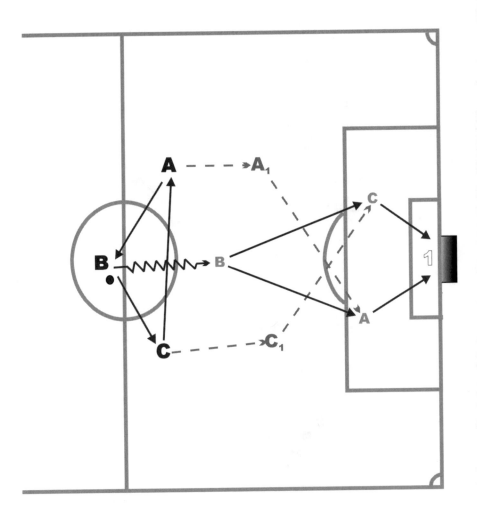

It starts as the basic exercise:

- B passes the ball to C;
- C passes it to A and goes to position C1;
- A passes it back to B and goes to position A1;
- B dribbles for a short distance, then he makes a prearranged sign; A and C criss cross to receive the pass and shoot at goal.

Even if we have not shown them in the Diagram, it is useful to add two marking players: in fact B should pass the ball to the teammate who has managed to free himself from his marker.

11. Technical-Tactical Exercise
Overlapping and Shot at Goal

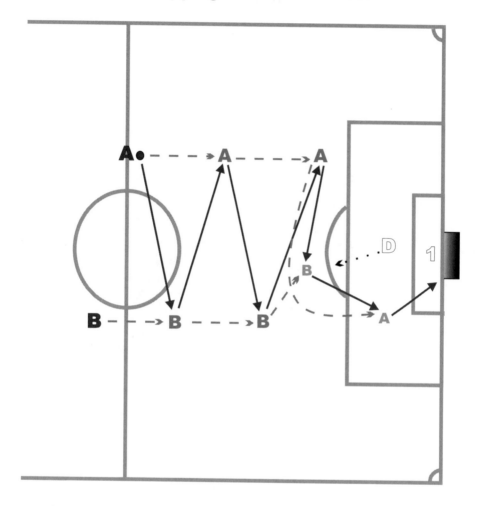

A and B pass the ball to each other (in a series of "triangulations") up to the edge of the penalty area.

After the last pass, A overlaps B, receives the pass from B then shoots at goal.

Then, B overlaps and shoots at goal.

This is the ideal movement in 2 versus 1 situations, as it also teaches the attacking players to avoid the off-side trap.

First the exercise will be carried out only by two attacking players, then we will add a defender at the edge of the penalty area: he can move forward to tackle the player making the last pass, trying to use the off-side tactics.

12. Technical-Tactical Exercise
Shot at Goal

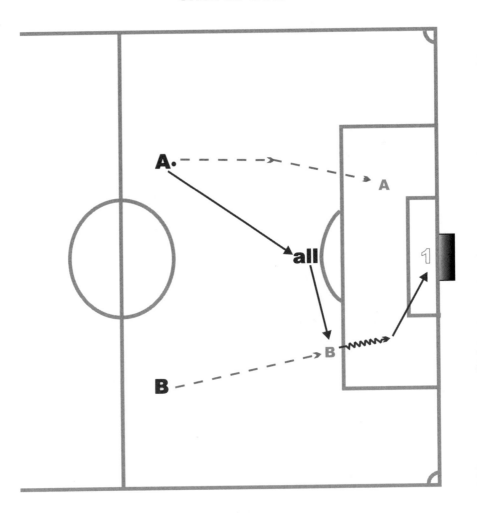

A or B passes the ball to the coach (all), or to another player; then both A and B run to the penalty area to receive the return pass.

The one who gets the pass dribbles the ball for some yards, then shoots at goal.

The player who does not get the ball continues to run towards the goalkeeper, thus getting used to making trouble in the opposing penalty area.

13. Physical-Technical Exercise
Shot at Goal

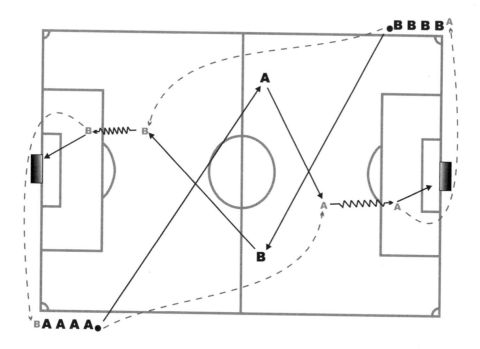

The shot at goal takes place after a 60 to 80-yard run increasing the speed.

The players are divided into two groups, and placed next to the diagonally opposite corners.

Two other players are placed in the midfield, on the side opposite to the one where their respective groups are.

The first player makes a pass to his teammate in the midfield, runs forward increasing the speed to receive the back pass in deep, and while running controls the ball then shoots at goal.

After the shot, he runs to the end of his line.

14. Tactical Exercise
Feint by a Forward to Free Himself for the Shot at Goal

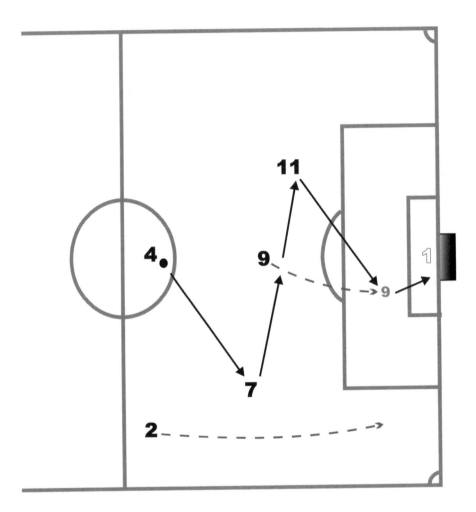

Game for the two forwards:

- 4 passes the ball to 7;

- 7 passes it to 9;

- with a feint, 9 lets the ball reach 11 and moves forward to "close the triangle", receiving the ball from 11 at the edge of the penalty area;

- 2 follows the action, overlapping 7 on the right wing.

15. Tactical Exercise
Criss-Crossings and Cut-ins to Set a Forward Free to Shoot at Goal

Game for the two forwards:

- 9 and 11 criss-cross;

- 7 moves onto the right wing;

- 8 passes the ball to 11, who has criss-crossed;

- now 11 waits for the movement of 7:
  a. 7 continues his penetration on the right, receives the pass from 11 and makes a cross pass to 9; or
  b. 7 cuts in, receives a back pass from 11, dribbles the ball and shoots at goal.

16. Tactical and Physical Exercise

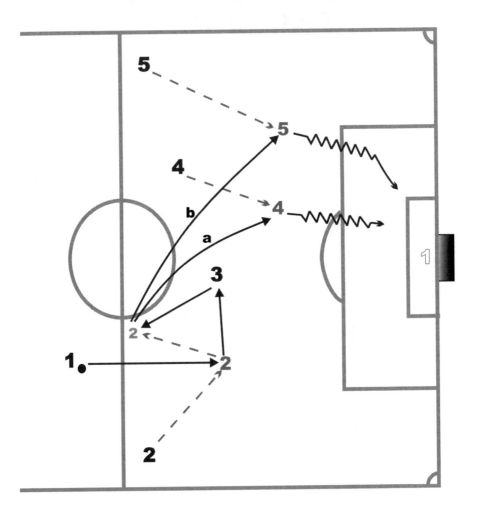

This exercise can be used as a warm-up for the final coaching session.

It can be carried out both with hands and with feet, both on a smaller and on a regular field.

- 1 passes the ball to 2 who has moved forward;
- 2 passes it to 3 and runs to get the back pass;
- once he has the ball, 2 can:
  - a. pass it to 4 who cuts in towards the center;
  - b. pass it to 5 who overlaps on the left wing;

- the player who gets the pass advances with the ball and then shoots at goal, while the other follows the action.

Then, 1 takes the place of 2; 2 takes the place of 3; 3 takes the place of 4. Two new players take the place of 1 and 5.

Variations to Exercise 16

We can add the criss-crossing between 4 and 5.
Later, we can add some backs: in this case, 4 and 5 can pass the ball to each other, or 4 can screen a back making room for 5, or vice versa, etc.

17. Physical-Technical Exercise
Cross Pass for the Goalkeeper's Interception

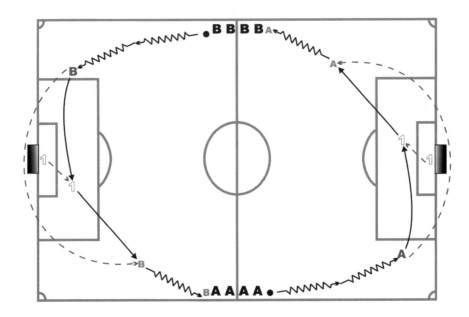

Two lines of players are in the midfield, near the sideline.

The first player of line A:

- dribbles the ball almost up to the end of the field;
- makes the cross pass which is intercepted by the goalkeeper;
- then sprints behind the goal and goes to receive the ball passed back to him by the goalkeeper;
- goes to the end of line B.

At the same time, the first player in line B does the same thing from the opposite side.

18. Physical and Technical-Tactical Exercise

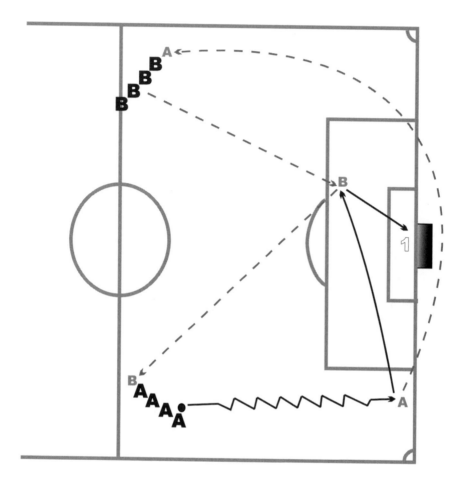

Two lines of players placed in the midfield.

The first player in line A dribbles the ball to the goal line and crosses the ball to the center of the penalty area to the first player of line B, who has advanced.

Then, the player of line A sprints behind the goal and goes to the end of line B.

The player of line B goes to the end of line A, cutting across the field.

19. Tactical Exercise
Passes and Overlaps Among Three Players

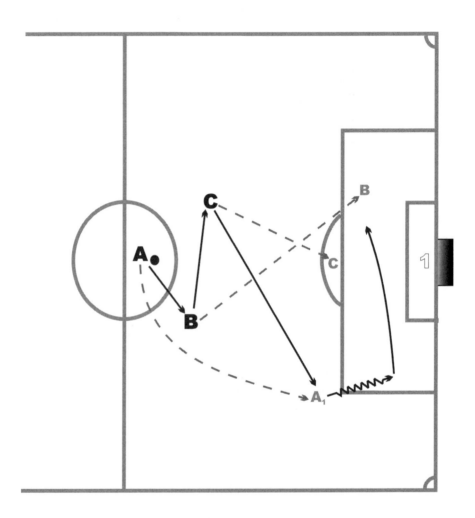

- A passes the ball to B and overlaps to position A1;

- B passes the ball to C;

- C makes a long pass to A, then runs forward to criss-cross with B;

- A dribbles with the ball towards the end of the field, then crosses the ball to B and/or C.

20. Technical Exercise
Attack and Defense on Cross Passes

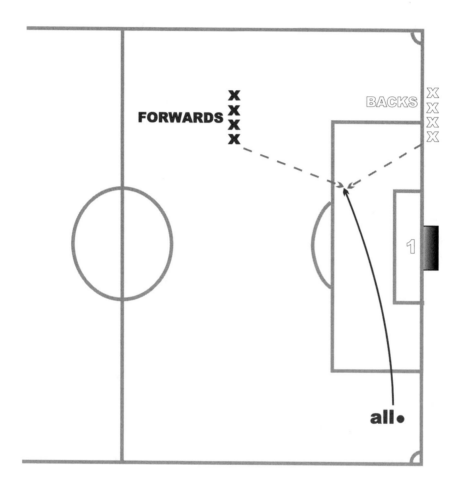

Place a line of forwards a few yards from the edge of the penalty area, and a line of backs just beyond the goal line.
The coach (all), or a player, makes a cross pass to the center of the penalty area: both the forward and the back try to intercept it, the former to score, the latter to prevent him from scoring.

21. Tactical Exercise
Overlapping on the Wings and Criss-Crossing

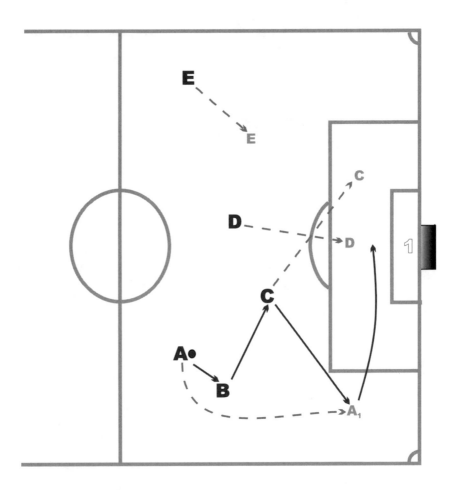

- A passes the ball to B and overlaps;
- B passes the ball to C, who immediately passes it to A who has reached position A1;
- C and D criss-cross and get into the penalty area;
- A crosses the ball to C and/or D;
- E closes the space towards the center.

22. Variation to Exercise 21

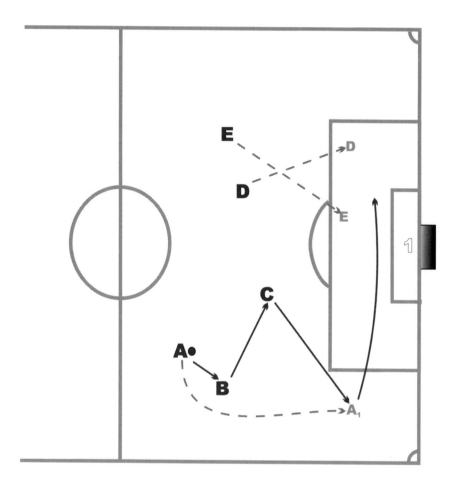

- A passes the ball to B and overlaps;
- B passes the ball to C, who immediately passes it to A who has reached position A1;
- E and D criss-cross and get into the penalty area;
- A crosses the ball to E and/or D.

23. Technical-Tactical Exercise
Getting Rid of Pressure

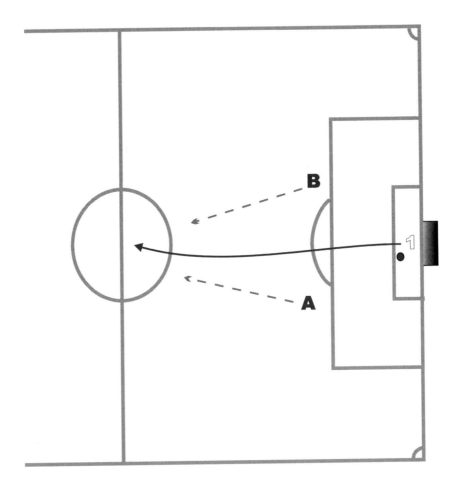

A and B are at the edge of the penalty area, facing the goalkeeper. The goalkeeper returns the ball to the midfield: A and B sprint to get to the ball.

The player who reaches the ball first will become the attacker: he will try to score after dribbling past the other player, who must defend.

24. Variation to Exercise 23

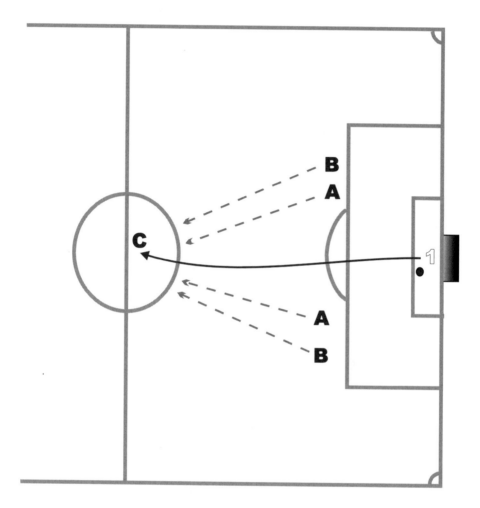

This time we have two pairs of players and player C in the midfield.

The players of the pair who gets the ball returned by the goalkeeper will become the attackers and will count on the help from C in a 3 versus 2 situation.

The other pair become defenders and will have to apply the off-side tactics.

25. Technical-Tactical Exercise
Avoiding Pressure in the Center

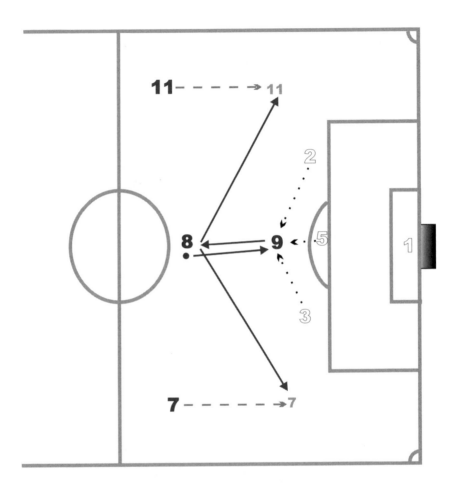

- 8 passes the ball to 9;

- pressed by backs 2, 5 and 3, 9 passes the ball back to 8;

- during this exchange, 7 and 11 moved onto their respective wings in order to receive the long pass from 8.

26. Tactical Exercise
Free Kick

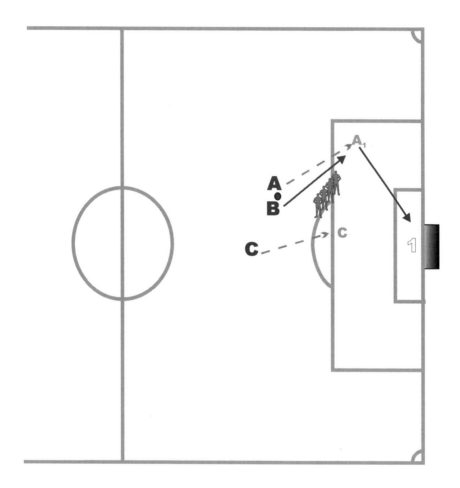

In front of the wall, players A and B are close to the ball while player C is slightly behind them, on their right.

C sprints forward as if he wants to get the ball and A feints to make a pass to him; instead, A sprints to position A1, where he gets the pass from B and shoots at goal.

Carry out the exercise also on the right with the players taking turns for the shot at goal.

27. Tactical Exercise
Free Kick

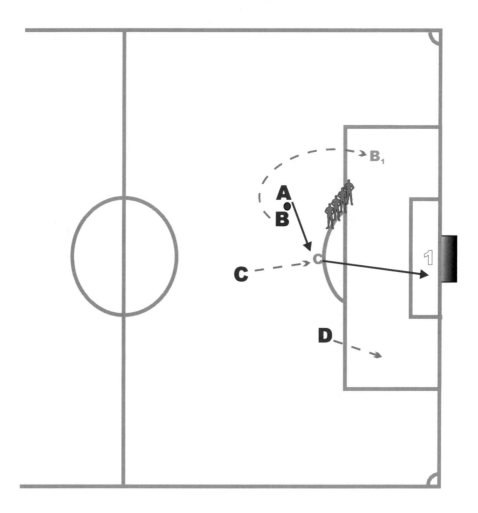

In front of the wall, players A and B are close to the ball while player C is slightly behind them, on their right.

Player D is further to the right, but almost along the same line as the wall.

Player B goes towards the ball, then suddenly changes his direction overlapping A and going to position B1. At this point, A goes towards the ball and feints to pass it to B1: instead, he makes a pass to C who has come forward and shoots at goal.

Eugenio Fascetti

Communication Between Coach and Players

Foreword

A good soccer coach does not only have to have technical-tactical knowledge: he must also be good at communicating it to his players.

This is particularly true for tactics: while skills are mostly instinctive and natural abilities, tactics must be assimilated clearly and interpreted rationally.

A clear explanation (by the coach) and a correct understanding (by the players) of the schemes of play are vital to the successful outcome of a game and to the performance in a whole season. Well, after several years' experience I have realized that the cause of many defeats lies in the lack of good technical-tactical communicating skills by the coach.

This is why I have decided to write a few pages about communication, hoping to be helpful to those who agree with me and to persuade those who do not.

Of course, the following pages contain just some advice, they are not a thesis on communication.

First Of All, A Humble Project

If we are used to saying "the players haven't understood me" or "that player hasn't understood me", then we should start asking:

"Why haven't I been understood?"

We must be ready to answer this question with a lot of objectivity, first of all by discussing our way of communicating.

In other words, the first thing to do is to check whether the misunderstanding depends on us: we should analyze our behavior, which requires humility but will certainly reap the rewards in the future.

THE NON-UNDERSTANDING OR INCORRECT UNDERSTANDING BY THE PLAYERS MAY DEPEND ON A WRONG WAY OF COMMUNICATING BY THE COACH. THEREFORE WE SHOULD ANALYZE OUR BEHAVIOR CAREFULLY, IN ORDER TO SPOT AND REMOVE THE CAUSES WHICH MAKE OUR COMMUNICATION INEFFECTIVE.

The Most Frequent Causes of Incorrect or Incomplete Communication

1. Missing or incorrect information on the program for the whole season

At the beginning of the pre-season conditioning, every good coach should know what he intends to do and how to go on for the whole season.

Even if many coaches have clear ideas about that, unfortunately either they keep them to themselves or explain them in a very brief way: this is a big mistake. In team-work (for soccer is such) all the group involved must know in advance the general work plan in its various phases.
In other words, all the group must be informed about:

- the goals;
- the time needed to reach them;
- the methods of working;
- the eventual problems that might be encountered.

The coach will have to pay a lot of attention to this first approach; then he must give the above information as clearly as possible, trying to make the players understand it clearly.

He will avoid a long talk which could end up in a long and boring monologue, by dividing the introduction of the general program into three or four brief moments in which the players will take part actively: he will involve them asking questions and removing doubts.

• Group involvement
This is an obstacle for many coaches; even if they try hard, they do not succeed in arousing interest and curiosity. Yet it is not so difficult to involve the listeners if we use some simple techniques.
For example, the coach may say:
"In every coaching session we will devote some minutes to the skills. But please, the exercises will have to be carried out with maximum seriousness and involvement, otherwise they will have no effect".
This is a very clear and intelligible message for everybody, yet it is not very stimulating or involving: those who listen cannot go any further than say that they have understood.

Instead, if the coach says the same thing by using a question:
"Do you think it is useful to devote some minutes to the skills in every coaching session?"
He will arouse a reaction from the players and will involve them.

He could also ask a single player:
"In your opinion, why is it useful to practice the skills regularly?"
You will see that all the other players will be curious to know the answer and will be willing to take part in the discussion.

In short, the coach can use the players themselves to pass on a message that he considers important: he does not pass it on as an "order" or a "principle", but by asking for the players' advice, thus stimulating and involving them.

• Motivation
This is a vital step in the communication between the coach and the players: when a person is motivated (which means also interested or made curious) he certainly pays more attention.

THE GENERAL PROGRAM MUST BE
COMMUNICATED CLEARLY
SO THAT ALL THE PLAYERS ARE FULLY AWARE OF IT.

COMMUNICATE IT IN AN INVOLVING WAY.

N.B. When the coach introduces the general program, he will underline the fact that it is not strict, but flexible and adaptable to the various necessities and circumstances that might arise. That is, the program might undergo variations and/or adaptations during the season.

2. Missing or incorrect preliminary information on the weekly and/or daily work plan

What we have said about the general program is as valid for the weekly or daily ones.
Some may object that in doing so we take time from concrete and practical work: this is not true, in fact during the coaching session many minutes are lost in explanations which could be saved if, before taking the field, the players were totally aware of:

- what they will have to do;
- why they will have to do it.

We can reach this aim only by informing them about ways and times of the coaching that we have planned for the whole week or for that single session.

NEVER FACE A WEEK AND/OR A SINGLE COACHING
SESSION WITHOUT PREVIOUSLY COMMUNICATING
THE PROGRAM TO THE PLAYERS.

---

3. Unclear exposition

a. "Table of reference"
We often communicate to a person without wondering whether he really understands what we are saying.
Many of us feel that we have clear ideas on a certain matter, so we think: "As I know well what I have to explain, I must certainly be clear and therefore understood".
Well, this is not completely true: in fact, if we do not have adequate communication skills, our ideas are likely to be clear only to us.

IT'S NO USE BEING EXPERTS ON TACTICS IF WE ARE NOT ABLE
TO COMMUNICATE AND TEACH IT TO OUR PLAYERS.

Even when we are certain that we have expressed our ideas clearly, they may not have been understood: this can happen first of all because the "table of reference" of the listener is not the same as the one of the speaker.

What do we mean by "table of reference"?
It is the matter or the idea we are referring to (or to which we want to draw somebody's attention).
Let's give an example: the coach explains a scheme in which there is:

- an overlapping of the side back;

- a criss-crossing between the forwards;
- a penetration of the midfielder.

The intention of the coach is above all to make the players understand the importance of the penetration of the midfielder: this is his "table of reference".

Instead, some players think that the coach wants to highlight the criss-crossing between the forwards: in this case the "table of reference" for some players is different from the one of the coach, and there will not be fruitful communication.

Before starting the explanation, it would be enough for the coach to say to the players:

"In this scheme there are different movements, but I want you to pay particular attention to the penetration of the midfielder".

What we have just said may seem obvious and taken for granted, but it really happens quite often that the coach starts talking without saying first what he wants to draw the players' attention to.

b. feed-back

We will deal with this further, when we introduce a practical teaching example and we deal with testing.

c. vocabulary

With the term "vocabulary" we mean "the words" that each one of us knows and uses. Therefore, to communicate with the others we need to use a vocabulary which must be understood by those who are listening to us.

This aspect is closely connected to the table of reference. In fact, the understanding of our listener is favored by the knowledge of the "table of reference" (that is the subject), but it may be inhibited later if we deal with the subject with words (that is, with a vocabulary) that the listener cannot understand.

This happens when:

1. We use technical terms without first explaining them to the players

Generally, the coach reads specific books, watches technical videos and attends qualified courses which enable him to learn all the technical expressions and terms that concern technical-tactical, psychological-physical, athletic and medical aspects of the soccer game.

Unlike him, the player is often quite inexperienced as far as technical terms, and he runs the risk of not understanding the vocabulary used by the coach when it gets too specific.

In order to avoid such difficulties in understanding, a coach must make sure during his explanations that a certain technical term is well known to all the players.

2. We use unfit and vague terms

This problem is the opposite of the previous one.

Sometimes, trying to be as communicative as possible, the coach may use a very inaccurate vocabulary, sometimes even slang.

It is true that this kind of immediate language can sometimes help draw the players' attention better, but only on rare occasions.

The coach must always use accurate and adequate terms, in correct English.

Last but not least, inappropriate language may also convey to the players a negative image of the coach.

d. syntax

While vocabulary concerns words, "syntax" refers to the whole sentence. If we talk using long sentences, with a series of conditional tenses, the structure of our syntax will be too complex and intricate and it will end up tiring or distracting those who should listen to us.

Let's give a couple of examples to show different ways to convey the same idea: in the first we will use a complex and intricate syntax, in the second a more explicit and easier one.

1. First example (complex syntax - not easily understandable) NO

"Our team being in the uncomfortable position of having to defend itself from a counterattack which, already superior in numbers, the opposing forwards are starting on the wing, a zone which in addition is wrongly defended by our linkman who has mistakenly got into the attack and so not in a position to return promptly, we will have to take the following measures...."

2. Second example (simple syntax - more understandable) YES

"Our opponents start a counterattack on the wing with superiority in numbers. Our linkman cannot return promptly, as he has moved into the attack. Let's see what measures we can take...."

e. digression

If while we talk about something we happen to jump from one subject to another it is because we do not finish expressing our idea: we wander from the point, following another idea that comes to our mind. In this way we end up getting mixed up and bewildering those who listen to us.

This can happen also to the coach, in particular when he has not prepared (even if only mentally) a list of the main points he would like to communicate: he speaks off the cuff, he improvises, he wanders from the point.

Explaining the tactics both of the role of a single player and of the whole team is quite complicated, as it involves actions and movements by many players, opponents included. Therefore, if the coach loses the thread of what he is saying, interrupting an argument and maybe returning to it later in his speech, the players will hardly absorb what he wants to communicate.

f. Way of speaking

The way and the tone of speaking cannot seriously prevent somebody from understanding what we mean.
Nevertheless, they can be influential on the listener's attention, which is often "caught" and involved also by the way of speaking and by the tone we use when we express our ideas.

Therefore, keep from:

1. using too many stock phrases: "that is...", "right?", "clear, isn't it?", "actually", "you know", and so on.

    I have met players who had fun counting all the "to the extent that..." and the "regardless of..." that their coach used in his explanations, instead of paying attention to what he was saying.

2. talking too quickly
    If somebody talks too quickly, the listener's attention will concentrate on the attempt to follow the words, thus ending up not understanding the ideas.

    Sometimes the words are uttered so quickly as to tumble out and become incomprehensible.

    Even if it is not easy, this defect can be corrected by learning to breathe with a more regular frequency.

3. talking too slowly, with long pauses in between words or sentences, or with a series of "er...", "ehm...", "eh..."

4. always using the same tone of voice.

A monotonous tone of voice generates boredom, as it flattens communication. The use of different tones makes for better communication: to lower and to suddenly raise one's voice is useful to underline and highlight what we want to say.
The listener is struck by the different tones of the voice, which stimulate his subconscious mind to memorize what has been said.

g. Taking for granted
When we explain some points, sometimes we do not clear up intentionally some detail (which may be relevant within our explanation) because we take for granted that the listener already knows it well.
This is a mistake: the explanation must be complete in every detail, with the assumption that the listener may not know or may not remember things that we have already talked about.

A Practical Example for Introducing and Explaining a Scheme of Play

In the next pages we are going to divide the introduction and the explanation into seven phases (or moments): anyway, this does not mean that you should do literally the same thing. In fact, we have carried out this division only for two reasons:

- to let you understand how important it is to set in order what we want to explain;

- for our greater convenience and clarity.

Each coach will be free to choose how to get organized.

1. INTRODUCTION OF THE GENERAL CONTEXT
(of the "table of reference") in which the scheme will have to be applied.
In this case, we need to introduce the scheme into our pattern of play, which the players should already know. Anyway, it will be useful to remind everybody once again.

2. EXPLANATION OF THE LOGISTICAL AND TECHNICAL-TACTICAL REASONS
Of course there are good reasons to propose a scheme to the players: they are both logistical and technical-tactical.
To be honest, there is no sharp distinction between logistical and technical-tactical reasons: we will keep them distinct for our convenience and for better understanding.

Examples of logistical reasons:
1. some players will miss the next matches, so their absence must be compensated for with a new scheme;

2. the next two matches will be played away and on smaller or much bigger fields than ours;

3. the condition of the field in winter does not enable us any longer to apply that particular scheme in which skills and speed are instrumental.

Examples of technical-tactical reasons:
1. characteristics of the next opponents;

2. the schemes we have applied so far are not very fruitful;

3. the scheme we are applying makes us expose ourselves too often;

4. the scheme we are applying has now been understood by all our opponents.

3. DESCRIPTION OF THE AIMS (OBJECTIVES) OF THE SCHEME

After explaining the reasons, we should explain the aims that we want to reach through the introduction of the scheme.

Let's not forget that the aims are not always only technical-tactical ("through this scheme we will try to solve the problem of the crowding of the midfield"), they often involve the player's psychological sphere ("this scheme will enable us to make good use of Smith's dribbling skills").

4. HINTS AT THE SINGLE PLAYERS' MOST IMPORTANT TASKS

We should not talk at length about the single players' most important tasks (we would end up making the player concentrate only on his specific task), yet some hints at what we expect of each one of them are needed.

For example: "we will see how the most delicate task in this scheme is given to the speed of reaction of the two forwards and of the ability of the side defender to adapt."
In this way the coach has hardly explained anything, yet he has probably aroused the curiosity of the forwards and of the side backs: they will certainly pay attention now, to listen to what they will have to do to apply the "speed of reaction" and the "ability to adapt".

5. INTRODUCTION BY DIAGRAMS
1. At first the players will be asked to look at the diagram of the complete scheme (it would be better to draw it before).

    It is better if the coach does not say anything, keeping silent while the players watch the scheme. After a while, some players will start making observations, even if in a low voice.

    This is the signal for you to start talking and ask: "What have you understood?" or "Is everything clear?"

You will get answers and/or comments, but do not expect these to be very well-organized: they are likely to be incomplete sentences, exclamations, attempts at explanation. Anyway, let them talk, then explain the scheme directly:

Using the already drawn diagram, show the movements and the actions of the single players.

It is helpful to use felt-tip pens or chalks of different colors to mark the movements (with or without the ball) and the passes of each single player involved in the scheme.

The attention of our listeners is attracted by the diagram, but is even greater if the player can "identify himself" with a particular color only for him.

N.B. The coaches often take for granted that all the players know and understand the symbols used for drawing schemes and exercises, but let's not forget that some players confuse the unbroken line indicating a pass with the dotted line used for the movement.

This is why we must first check if all the symbols are clear for good understanding.

Besides, some coaches do not "draw" in the same way: some use "X" to indicate a back and "O" to indicate a forward, others a triangle or a square, respectively. Some do not use a symbol for the possession of the ball. Some do not indicate the player as he moves: they just indicate him once, at the start, then leave it up to the player's imagination. Sometimes these movements are indicated with a dotted circle. Therefore, during the first technical-tactical session we must explain to the players what symbols and marks we are going to use.

2. Now, leaving within sight the diagram we have just explained, let's take another piece of paper or another black board and let's draw once more all the movements and the actions of the single players involved in the scheme (let's not forget that each player has been given a color).
    Thus, we will reproduce the whole original diagram.

3. At this point we can explain the whole scheme again.

6. CHECK
1. Questions

Up to now we have explained - as clearly as possible - hoping to be understood.

But have we really been understood? Let's check that.

When we check whether our players have understood we must also check whether they have listened. This is important to assess our way of explaining things (which can also be defined as way of teaching).

In other words, we must check the feed-back: we have sent out a signal and now we expect a "return signal".

The feed-back is important in every kind of communication, particularly in our field as the explanation must absolutely be understood in order to apply the scheme.

The ideal situation would be a spontaneous feed-back, with the players directly asking questions or expressing doubts.

But this rarely happens, so we must stimulate the feed-back through questions aimed at checking at the same time:
- if there has been feed-back;
- if the players have understood us.

Of course, the questions must be related to our explanation, for example "which player do you think plays an instrumental role in the scheme?"

If there is no question to our answer or if the answer bears no relation to our explanation there has been no feed-back.

N.B.
An answer which is inaccurate but somehow relating to our explanation is a positive feed-back.

Instead, the questions aimed at checking if the players have understood what we said must be more accurate: in particular, we should check:

- if the single player's tasks have been understood.

We will ask questions like "imagine you are player 2, what must you do?", "in your opinion, what is the most important thing in the movements of the side back?";

- if the single player can link up his task to the whole scheme.

We will ask questions like "what is player 10 supposed to do while you move onto the right wing?", "What can be the reaction of the opponent who marks the teammate you are passing the ball to?"

N.B.
Our questions must check whether our communication has been clear: the answers share the same aim, they must be used to judge the players ("you have understood", "you have misunderstood", "you have not paid attention", etc.).
If the answers are positive on the whole (that is, if most players show that they have understood), we will go on to the next point.

2. Correction and clearing up
Correction and clearing up should be made in a different language from the one used in the explanation we have just given.

The fact is that the player may have misunderstood because we may have used words or ideas that he could not understand.

I have heard coaches say: "I have explained the scheme five times and some players still have not understood it", to find out later that all five times the explanation was given in the same way and with the same words.

If I say to the back: "you must not make that movement uninspiredly and repeatedly" and he does not understand, it is no use repeating the same words many times: he will never understand. I will have to use other words, for example "you must not make the same movement mechanically, always in the same way, try to use some imagination".
As in the example, a player can have difficulty in understanding some words: when he has difficulty in understanding a whole idea, we should provide him with practical examples or roundabout expressions.

3. Criticism
Even when we say that we are ready to accept criticism, it is not a pleasure to be subject to it: none of us likes to see his opinions and theories criticized.

Some coaches think that allowing the players to criticize is a sign of weakness and of uncertainty: "I have made this decision because I have thought deeply about it, now I cannot reopen the whole question just because my theories do not meet the theories of some player...".

Our opinion is that criticism must not be refused, as its acceptance is like an incentive which prompts us to go over our theories.

That is, we must take note of criticism as it can help us to be clearer and more convincing.

From this point of view, the objection raised by a player can be turned to our own advantage if we give the impression of listening to it and appreciating it.

Let's see a concrete example.

One coach refuses criticism: his players know it and so they take good care not to say anything, partly because they are afraid of not being first-string players any more if they criticize something.

So, some of those players take the field and apply the coach's directions while thinking that they can be partly or totally wrong.

Are you certain that their performance will be optimal? I doubt it.

If those players had the chance to express their opinions freely and to get explanations their performance would be more effective and responsible.

Listening to and discussing eventual criticism puts the coach in an advantageous position, as he "delegates" a part of responsibility to his players.

Anyway, generally a player does not feel up to contradicting his coach, either for self-interest or because he is shy or he feels nervous: in this case it is up to the coach to demand criticism. Yet, even if he asks his players to express their opinions, he must be careful not to give the impression that he refuses criticism or nothing will come out of it. Such impression of refusal is conveyed by spontaneous reactions which are very hard to control: upset, nervous, uneasy gestures and looks that the others notice immediately.

Let's see a couple of practical examples:

Example 1

The player makes a critical observation which is not to the point at all, almost "silly".

The coach can answer in two different ways:

Wrong way: "it seems to me quite a trite...meaningless observation". Or: "I cannot figure out what this observation has to do with my explanation".

In this way we humiliate the player: he will take good care not to make any other observation or to ask any other question, especially if he is shy. We run the risk of cutting off any form of communication with him.

Right way: "even if this observation does not sound too pertinent...too accurate, I am glad that you have made it because it helps me to pin-point better....".

In this way we lay emphasis on his intervention while sincerely admitting that it was not pertinent.

Example 2

The player makes a pertinent observation.

In this case we can also answer in two different ways:

Wrong way: "this observation may also be right, but this is not the right moment to discuss it...".

The intention to "cut short" in order to avoid criticism is much too evident.

Right way: "this objection is right. We will take it into consideration at the proper time...".

We give satisfaction to the player who has made the observation, while at the same time taking time to think about it.

If the observation is really logical and forces us immediately to make clear what we have explained, we will answer:

"I expected this observation: I hoped somebody would make it, as it shows that you have really paid attention...".

Then we will make clear the idea.

After the discussion, we will move to the field to carry out what we have explained:

- a. we will show the scheme again (do not forget to carry with you a board or a paper with the diagram);

- b. we will assign the starting positions;

- c. we will show the movements and the actions of the single players (without the ball);

- d. we will show the team movement (without the ball);

- e. then we will introduce the ball:

- f. we will carry out the scheme on a smaller field, using the hands;

- g. then we will carry out the scheme on a smaller field, with the feet;

- h. then on a regular field, using the hands;

i.   finally on a regular field, with the feet.

N.B.
When the players become familiar with the method of teaching we will skip some points: for example, we will skip point **a** to go directly to point **b**, then to **d**, **f** and **h**.
We will skip some points also when we must explain very easy schemes.

Checking, correcting and clearing up must be carried out with the same attitude and method used for the theoretical introduction.
When we need to correct the wrong movement of a player on the field, we should first of all show him the diagram of the scheme: correcting and understanding will be easier.

If we have a video camera, it will be extremely helpful to tape the scheme while it is carried out and then watch it all together through a video cassette recorder, stopping the tape to explain and correct mistakes.

Index

Other Books from REEDSWAIN

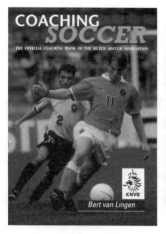

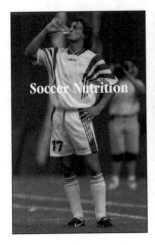
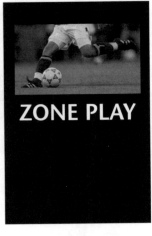
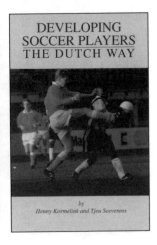
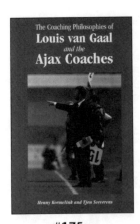
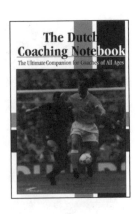